MIRED

Life in the Swamp

◆

Ruminations on the Irrelevance of Truth in an Age of Unreason, Lies, and Killer Pandemics

---

W. E. Gutman

CCB Publishing
British Columbia, Canada

Mired: Life in the Swamp – Ruminations on the Irrelevance
of Truth in an Age of Unreason, Lies, and Killer Pandemics

Non-fiction. Essays. History. Current events.

Copyright ©2021 by W. E. Gutman
ISBN-13 978-1-77143-467-6
First Edition

Library and Archives Canada Cataloguing in Publication
Title: Mired : life in the swamp : ruminations on the irrelevance of truth
in the age of unreason, lies, and killer pandemics / W.E. Gutman.
Other titles: Life in the swamp : ruminations on the irrelevance of truth in the
age of unreason, lies, and killer pandemics | Ruminations on the irrelevance of
truth in the age of unreason, lies, and killer pandemics
Names: Gutman, W. E., 1937- author.
Description: First edition.
Identifiers: Canadiana (print) 20210098716 | Canadiana (ebook) 20210098783
| ISBN 9781771434676 (softcover) | ISBN 9781771434683 (PDF)
Subjects: LCSH: Civilization, Modern—21st century. | LCSH: Civilization, Modern—Philosophy.
| LCSH: Political science—Philosophy. | LCSH: Ideology. | LCSH: Culture—Philosophy.
Classification: LCC CB430 .G88 2021 | DDC 909.83—dc23

Cover design by the author.
Photograph on the cover is in the public domain.

This book is printed on acid-free paper.

Disclaimer by author: References to real persons, alive or dead, are contextual and crucial to
the narrative. Some names have been changed to protect the identity of certain individuals.

Fair Use Notice: This work contains minor excerpts, with attribution, the use of which has not
always been specifically authorized by the copyright owner. It is believed this constitutes a
"fair use" of any such copyrighted material, as provided for in Section 107 of the US Copyright
Law.

Extreme care has been taken by the author to ensure that all information presented in this book
is accurate and up to date at the time of publishing. The publisher cannot be held responsible
for any errors or omissions. Additionally, neither is any liability assumed by the publisher for
damages resulting from the use of the information contained herein.

Publisher: CCB Publishing
              British Columbia, Canada
              www.ccbpublishing.com

TO THE RIVER AND TO THE FERRYMAN

Only two things are infinite, the universe and human stupidity,
and I'm not sure about the former.
—Albert Einstein

♦

The apocalypse is not something which is *coming*.
It has arrived in major portions of the planet. It is only because we live
in a bubble of incredible privilege and social insulation
that we still have the luxury of anticipating the apocalypse.
—Terence McKenna

♦

Donald Trump is not a curious person. He barely reads, if at all.
[His] sheer level of intellectual laziness is astounding.
—Anonymous*

♦

A wise man can play the part of a clown,
but a clown can't play the part of a wise man.
—Malcolm X

♦

In the US, there's basically one party: The business party.
—Noam Chomsky

---

* Miles Taylor, former Homeland Security official in the Trump administration and the much-maligned author of *A Warning* © 2019, Hachette.

IN THE BEGINNING CAME THE END—Some stories, to make sense, must start at the end because what happens next is either forgotten, redacted, refuted, doctored, or buried in the boneyard of revisionism. The end I allude to is a *culmination* rather than a *finale*. It's the inevitable climax of fateful events whose origins and predictability can be glimpsed only through the prism of hindsight. Cyclical and repetitive, such high points imply that the past and the present are one, that endings are pregnant with embryonic beginnings, some monstrous in their deformities, each self-destined, each capable of changing the course of history. It was this epiphany, felt at a time of great turmoil in Amerika* that prompted many of us, after four years of lunacy, to ask a number of troubling questions: Is President Donald J. Trump, an unhinged con man contemptuous of democracy, plotting a *"putsch"*—a coup d'état? Are his arrogance, petulant, despotic mien, his eagerness to stir confusion and incite violence deliberate electoral stratagems? Or are they the devices of a deranged, politically suicidal dilettante? After all, these ploys, which included dishing out a grotesque and malodorous bouillabaisse of falsehoods about Amerika's *"values"* (translation: the *"splendor"* of slavery and the virtues of white supremacy) had served him well when he first ran for office. Curiously, maddeningly, they beguiled a large chunk of voters as he bulldozed his way to seek a second term. Or was Trump a deflection? Was something sinister brewing, unnoticed, behind the scenes, whose origins and objectives might not have been known—if at all—until it was too late? No matter what happens, we surmised, Amerika would never be the same.

Against all odds, former Vice-President Joe Biden triumphed. People danced in cities around the country and the world. Church bells rang jubilantly in Paris. Bruised, democracy prevailed. But as Shakespeare warned in Julius Caesar, *"The evil*

---

* The America I once knew is no more. Welcome to *Amerika*.

1

that men do lives after them." Despair, rancor, and a taste for bluster contributed to Trump's meteoric popularity ... and infamy. The gaping and purulent wound that Trumpism inflicted will take time to heal. Bitter, his followers can be expected to poison whatever is left of the future.

◆

I don't know about you but I'm old enough to remember Adolf Hitler's tirades as throngs of drooling admirers crammed Berlin's huge *Sportpalast* arena, and Benito Mussolini's snooty, jaw-jutting harangues from atop his balcony overlooking Rome's Piazza Venezia. Powerful orators, both posed as patriots while telling lies and spitting venom. Did Trump's strident but inarticulate pledges to make *"Amerika Great Again,"* (a utopian Valhalla that never was) lead to unmendable discord, as did a litany of ominous and incoherent pleas to repel a mythical *"socialist"* fifth column poised to lay waste to the nation? Did *"the leader of the Free World"* and his adoring storm troopers believe that US history is proprietary and that retelling it includes the right to infuse it with untruths, distortions, and self-aggrandizing fictions? Witness Trump's weepy gripe:

> *"We grew up with a certain history, and now they're trying to change it. That's why they want to take down our monuments. That's why they want to take down our statues."*

◆

Answers to these questions inevitably spawned a new subset of postmortems, all alarming: Why did the spineless members of Trump's administration refuse to acknowledge what scientists call a *"staggering rise in natural disasters"* that they attribute to the climate crisis? Why aren't political and business leaders taking robust action to mitigate the impact of climate change and stop the planet from turning into *"an uninhabitable hell for millions of people?"*

Meanwhile, the coronavirus pandemic which, at this writing, has killed more than 1.3 million and afflicted at least 60 million worldwide, has exposed Amerika's failure to prevent a new wave of deaths and illnesses despite repeated early warnings from health experts. Why do so many people continue to insist that Covid-19 is either a hoax or a plague concocted in some secret leftist lab? Why this lunatic inclination to believe absurdities?

We all know why white supremacists worship Trump. But how can otherwise good people stomach him? Is it because they were forced from childhood to believe in fairy tales? *"Show me a person who believes in Noah's ark,"* says writer David Bowles, *"and I'll show you a Trump voter."*

THE PUNCH & JUDY SHOW—And then came the Great Debate, the first televised gladiatorial duel between incumbent Trump and contender Joe Biden, which put an end to the questions we asked by legitimizing all the anxieties that consumed us over the past four years: The fragile state of democracy and the eroding influence of a vulgar, unscrupulous individual, a dangerous psychopath who belongs in a straitjacket behind padded walls. What will be remembered most from this debate is Trump's combative, crimson-faced rictus, his flights from reality, and his threat that the election will *"not end well."* We will never know whether he was foretelling his downfall or threatening violence. He refused to concede defeat should he lose. He declined to condemn white supremacists, telegraphing instead a far-right group, the Proud Boys, to *"stand back and stand ready."* Amerika was being given the alarming foretaste of what four more years of Trumpism would have brought to a gravely wounded Amerika.

The second "debate" offered more of *this* and less of *that*, but enough of the *same* to conclude that Trump, a consummate prevaricator and raging pit bull, remains unfazed by the truth. He kept lying and blitzing his opponent with disjointed, repetitious, and meaningless claims maddeningly out of context with the issues at hand.

◆

At the time, with five weeks until the election, the televised debates between Trump and Joe Biden hardened all the concerns that arose over the preceding four years. The most striking moments of this chaotic and brutal confrontation between two septuagenarians were not Biden's exasperated exclamations in response to an uncouth, pugnacious man who kept interrupting him and whom he called a *"clown."* Nor was it the personal attacks on business made abroad by his opponent's son. What will be remembered from this encounter was Trump's chilling warning: *"It's not going to end well."*

Once again, Trump cast doubt on the validity of the presidential election and the anticipated avalanche of mail-in ballots occasioned by the Covid-19 pandemic. The president's ambiguity over the conduct of the election was just as disturbing as his refusal to expressly condemn the violence of white supremacists when he was urged to do so by the journalist leading the debate. Instead, Trump, his face twisted in a sardonic smile, enigmatically threatened violence.

This repudiation of civism by a US president left us stunned. On the form, Trump's aggressiveness and indiscipline during these ninety-minute verbal skirmishes did not surprise those who followed his antics since his first election campaign: He led the debate as if it were a tweeting session, with invective, self-glorification, and gratuitous accusations, and without the slightest scruple. Democrats seemed to be miffed, but the president's base savored his combativeness. It is to this electorate that he turned, to remobilize it, perhaps deputize it, while poll after poll indicated he was losing ground.

On the substance, the president's casualness over the electoral process, in parallel with his attacks on public services and the freedoms he took with institutions during his first term, must be sobering. Four years of Trumpism have largely contributed to weakening one of the world's largest democracies. It's a national embarrassment and a bitter lesson.

Highly anticipated abroad, the debates were a reflection of the year 2020, challenging for the whole world but particularly politically difficult in the US: It began with a disastrous impeachment trial of the president and followed by urban violence reflecting, in the midst of the pandemic, the growing polarization of society.

We were all hoping for a crushing defeat at the polls (which we feared might ignite widespread civil unrest). We also knew that, ultimately, Amerika didn't need Trump, his acolytes in the Senate, his armed goons, Russia, or Iran to rig elections. The Electoral College, a master illusionist, we dreaded, could turn a crushing rout into a miraculous victory.

A FIELD OF RUINS—Democratic candidate Joe Biden defeated President Donald Trump. The recounts of votes have been completed; his rival's appeals, after long and often loutish theatrics, were purged. Biden will move into the White House on January 20, 2021.

It would be a big mistake to settle for a collective sigh of relief. After four years of a devastating mandate, a few months of a demeaning campaign, and days, or weeks of a dismaying legal-political guerrilla war, Biden, tasked with rebuilding everything or almost everything, will step into the field of ruins abandoned by his predecessor. To do so, he will have to stay calm, as he did when Trump baited fanatical cliques to engage in civil confrontations, and when ambulance-chasing lawyers tried to impugn the validity of legal paper ballots. Above all, he must avoid getting distracted by the stream of frenzied, deceitful, and manipulative Tweets that the outgoing president is expected to send before and after Biden's inauguration. Anything but unpredictable, Trump will no doubt continue until the last day of his presidency, and long after, to behave like a black hole of self-centeredness that would rather engulf democracy, the country, and the planet rather than acknowledge defeat and a surfeit of sins.

Since the presidential election of November 3, Trump has consistently striven to rise to the height of his caricature— that of a man devoured by ego, unable to recognize defeat, ready to weaken the institutions he had sworn to protect for the sole purpose of appeasing his resentment. The presidency of the world's leading power does not change a man but reveals what he is. The image Trump projects is devastating. The norms he attacked were those in which the US takes pride: Acknowledging the rival's victory and assisting in the peaceful transfer of power from one party to another. The loser's concession speech and the letter left on the Resolute Desk of the

Oval Office by the outgoing president to his successor have long been seen as evidence of the maturity and solidity of a democracy in which personal ambition fades when the imperative of the common good is at hand.

A president on departure can of course adopt symbolic measures to consolidate his legacy. But Donald Trump's attitude is less about polishing his political legacy than about undermining the authority of the future president. For this, if nothing else, history should reserve its harshest criticism.

Yes, he could run a second time but would face serious obstacles. The first would be political: Nonplused, the Republican Party might be tempted to turn the page on Trumpism. The question of age might also arise: He would be 78. He would also face legal challenges. In New York, he is the subject of two investigations that could each result in prosecution. The first, criminal and initiated by the Manhattan district attorney, Cyrus Vance, targets possible acts of tax evasion, insurance fraud, and accounting falsifications. In September 2020, the New York Times revealed that he had paid only $750 in taxes in 2016. Last, a civil lawsuit launched by New York State Attorney Letitia James seeks to determine whether the Trump Organization lied about the size of its assets to obtain loans and tax benefits. Thus, Trump's judicial horizon could darken greatly as he leaves the White House and instantly loses his presidential immunity.

Inquisition as such, that is, apart from methods and severity of results, has remained a live institution. It is not farfetched to imagine an inquisitorial reign should Trump seek reelection. What is curious about dictatorships is that despite their powerful means of repression they secretly fear the slightest murmur of dissent. One can easily imagine, despite the bombast, the constant state of agitation that Trump must be in.

Golf, prison, TV shows, a second run for the White House? Nothing is certain about Donald Trump's future. In any case, Amerika's 45th president will continue to make a name for himself, a name that history is not likely to exalt.

♦

Stymied by the speed and chaotic nature of unfolding events, unable to predict with any degree of accuracy how I might wrap up this work, I faced three choices: Shelve the manuscript until inauguration; rework it from scratch by assuming the unlikely rebirth of democracy following a fervently longed and spectacular Trump defeat; or proceed with it as is. I chose the latter. Past is prologue. It serves as a backdrop to the self-scripted science-fiction nightmare that has now entrapped us all.

♦

I now return to my previously scheduled narrative. Before you turn the page, consider this: One can rationalize the election of a scoundrel; how does one justify the imbecility of 73 million voters?

PAST IS PROLOGUE—Heat. Humidity. Unrelenting. Merciless. If the air, which has a boggy odor of jungle rot, were any damper, you could drink it. Yesterday, the air-conditioner died. Welcome to the Swamp.

♦

I began compiling the ensuing essays at a time of quasi-normalcy — that is, if we ignore four years of an aberrant, pompous, corrosive, and shockingly mediocre presidency, the socio-economic and cultural tremors it engendered, the daily lies, aberrations, threats, and vengeful decrees that further cleaved an already disunited United States. Above the din of partisan politics, and aside from the occasional anecdotes we exchanged, my friends and I talked about Donald J. Trump, a man who rejects the advice of experts, fires those who contradict him, and replaces decency with a moral system that reflexively scapegoats the weak and the vulnerable. We spoke of catabolic capitalism [the process by which an organism devours itself]; the tenuous but tantalizing possibility of intelligent life beyond Earth (I'm a skeptic. Nature couldn't possibly have made the same mistake twice); man's paradoxical propensity for virtue and wickedness; environmental degradation, global warming, and climate change; the rise and fall of empires; *"God"* and religion; life in the Swamp; the role of journalism in an era of *"fake news;"* racism, antisemitism, Jews, Israel, and the Palestinians; human rights, and genocide; the irreconcilable chasm between genius and stupidity; the death of democracy; Amerika; the next Permian extinction; and the *Haskalah.**

---

* Jewish Enlightenment. Arising in the 1770s, the movement was doomed to failure. Freethinking and religion are mutually exclusive. Jews would have had to make room for concepts that are fundamentally hostile to mysticism. Ethnic considerations aside, a Jew, by definition, is someone who practices Judaism. You cannot have your cake and eat it too.

We even wondered out loud whether, long overdue, a novel and deadly scourge might silently stir to life after a long incubation and decimate large numbers of people across the globe. Nature may be indifferent, but it is self-aware and self-regulating, we agreed, and it reacts against the abuses that threaten its fragile equilibrium. We also posited that overpopulation and the attendant assault by man on his environment imperil his survival, and we concluded that nature would even out the score by liquidating as many of its most perfidious miscreation — Homo sapiens — as possible in a final act of retributive self-immolation.

And lo and behold, just as we were about to abscond from the Swamp, a new and wily virus blossomed, dispersing its poisoned spores, sending dozens, then hundreds, then thousands to hospitals and morgues, spreading panic, inspiring frenzied exhortations to wash hands, wear masks, and observe "social distancing" protocols in the midst of a countervailing public revolt against such life-saving conventions. And we looked, transfixed and dumbfounded at yet another display of criminal stupidity as thousands of youths, believing themselves immortal, flocked to free-for-all parties over spring break and the July 4th weekend while the pandemic was raging, none wearing masks, none keeping their distance, all clustering about and wigwagging like demented macaques, all consciously if not deliberately inviting infection, suffering, and death.

THE DAYS OF WHINE AND RUSES—A year into the pandemic, the US continues to endure the worst coronavirus outbreak in the developed world. Considerable blame belongs to an inept and often muddled federal response that would be met with terror, confusion, and criminal laxity. Meanwhile, posturing haughtily à la Mussolini (or spitting venom à la Hitler) before doting fans, affecting self-confidence while moaning about the media, *"hoaxes,"* and *"enemies of the people,"* Trump was reassuring the nation:

> *"We have it totally under control. It's one person coming in from China, and we have it under control. It's going to be just fine. One day it's like a miracle, it will disappear."*

He then proceeded to cook up strategies that would strip citizens of their rights and freedoms and threatening to punish those who stood in his way.

Then came the televised premeditated and ignominious murder of George Floyd by a Minneapolis cop who kept his hands in his pockets and stared blankly at the camera while a gasping Floyd begged for his life. That would soon be followed by the worst civil unrest since the assassination of Martin Luther King, Jr. and the televised savage beating of the late Rodney King in Los Angeles, and by the election of far-right self-avowed islamophobes and conspiracy theorists, whom Trump endorsed.

In her tell-all book, the president's niece, Mary Trump, describes her uncle as being much as he was at three years old—incapable of growing, learning, or evolving, unable to regulate his emotions, modulate his responses, or taking and synthesizing information. Instead,

> *"... Donald withdrew to his comfort zones – Twitter, Fox News – casting blame from afar, protected by a figurative or literal bunker. He rants about the weakness of others even as he demonstrates his own. But he can never escape the fact that he is and always will be a*

terrified little boy. Donald's monstrosity is the manifestation of the very weakness within him that he's been running from his entire life."

And the quasi-normalcy to which we had become grudgingly habituated turned to chaos, fear, and lunacy.

SCIENCE-FICTION MIGHTMARE—Suddenly, everybody invoked the Constitution, some to awaken Amerika's troubled conscience by reaffirming its noblest ideals, others to justify their First Amendment right to reject them. So much for the rule of law and egalitarian principles. On the eve of Amerika's 244th anniversary as a nation, I looked back at its infancy. On July 2nd, 1776, the Continental Congress voted to declare independence from the British monarch, King George III. The actual Declaration of Independence was signed two days later, on July 4th. The declaration, authored principally by Thomas Jefferson, was a visionary document that set the country's history and capitalist future in motion. In his original draft, Jefferson wrote:

"We hold these truths to be sacred & undeniable, that all men are created equal & independent, that from that equal creation they derive rights inherent & inalienable, among which are the preservation of life, & liberty, & the pursuit of happiness..."

Further down in the document, after a long list of grievances, Jefferson blamed the king for waging,

"cruel war against human nature itself, violating its most sacred rights of life & liberty in the persons of a distant people who never offended him, captivating & carrying them into slavery..."

Jefferson—ironically, a slaveholder himself—goes on and on in a similar vein, the most extended single idea of the declaration. But this passage was deleted from the final version by the Continental Congress ... and slavery, which would fester for another 250 years, ended up not being mentioned at all. That seemingly inconsequential decision, which ultimately drove the US to civil war and to the brink of disunion, has been omitted from school history curricula as well.

In Lincoln's Gettysburg address we find the phrase *"and dedicated to the proposition that all men are created equal."* By *"all men"* I must assume Lincoln meant all of humanity. But a proposition is a statement or assertion that expresses a judgment or opinion. It's a recommendation, which, by inference and intent implies a certain degree of uncertainty relative to its merits or likelihood of universal acceptance. It's wishful thinking. When someone proposes, someone else disposes ... and not always to the proposer's satisfaction.

Both Jefferson and Lincoln understood the tactical value of rhetorical flourish. But both were wrong or disingenuous: Men are not, never have been, never will be *"created equal."* That claim is, at best, a cruel ploy. We are born rich or poor, stupid, or smart, healthy, or prone to disease, creative and talented or intellectually sterile. We are then further separated by social and cultural status, by the lies our parents tell us, by race, skin color, and religion. And we lose all freedom and individuality when we seek (or are forced) to follow the flock. The only equality we share is a universal close-ended destiny.

The notion, recently revived, that the socio-economic and political character of what would become the US was forged in August 1619, when the first slave ship landed in Virginia, and not on July 4, 1776, when the colonists declared independence from Britain, is something that many in Amerika find hard to swallow. But slavery is what fueled Amerika's economy for 250 years and this monstrosity indeed began in August 1619 when 30-40 African men and women in shackles weakened by disease and a long sea voyage were sold and consigned to a life of unending toil, abuse, and premature death. Initiated by the New York Times, the 1619 Project continues to stir controversy because it upsets the contrived but widely accepted *"creation myth"* of the founding of the US, which handsomely profited countless generations of European descent while destroying the lives of generations of Native tribes, slaves, and their descendants.

♦

Predictably, serving red meat as bait to his political base in preparation for the presidential election, Trump banned federal agencies from conducting race-sensitivity training related to *"white privilege"* and *"critical race theory"* that he claimed amounts to *"divisive, anti-patriotic propaganda."* This revisionist ruse follows a pattern by the president of disparaging attempts to process or reckon with the country's troubled racial history.

The week before California began to burn all over again, what was happening? Amerika was diving head-first into an authoritarian abyss. The President did everything over those last few weeks from sending storm troopers to bash heads and gas people in the streets, to having secret police shanghai protesters, to proclaiming he wouldn't give up power peacefully, to openly building a political dynasty, to sending his kids to bully the nation into submission.

None of this, though, should have been a surprise. Amerika's police routinely killed hated minorities. Caught on video. This one strangled, that one suffocated, the other shot in the back. The world was aghast. What had America become? It had become *Amerika*, a pre-authoritarian state after making an abortive attempt at being a true democracy, which only lasted about thirty years. Before that, it was the world's largest apartheid state.

We should be careful not to rhapsodize the Founding Fathers. The liberty, equality, and justice they advocated were self-directed and narrow, not universal. They were all monopolistic landowners dedicated to capitalist ideals, including the *"right to property"* which, by its very essence, excludes those who own nothing and those from whom that property was stolen. They all had slaves. One of Jefferson's policies was to push Native tribes to the other side of the Mississippi River and to kill those who resisted. The Constitution is a telling document that should be understood by what it does not say. When the Founding Fathers wrote ... *"to establish Justice, insure domestic Tranquility, provide for the common defense, promote the general Welfare, and secure the Blessings of Liberty to ourselves and our Posterity,"* they meant for *"us"*—White Anglo-Saxon Protestants proprietors--not *them*, for the white privileged classes, not the low-born landless masses, the slaves, or the indigenous peoples they dispossessed and massacred.

To those who claim that Amerika *"has changed,"* I argue that after a long and muted but troubled slumber, Amerika revealed itself for what it always was: bigoted, xenophobic, homophobic, misogynistic, greedy, at once pretentiously puritanical and insatiably promiscuous, hopelessly provincial, and belligerent. President Jimmy Carter recently noted that in its 244-year history, Amerika had enjoyed only sixteen years of peace, making it, as he wrote, *"the most warlike nation in the history of the world."* Since 2001, the US has spent over $6 trillion on military operations and war, money that should have been invested in domestic priorities. It took the election and reelection of the first Black president to lift the mask and expose Amerika's ugly face for all to see: The mythical image that the US has of itself (and which it shamelessly trumpets around the world) is a propagandist lie that many are dedicated to preserve. Says Barak Obama in his 768-page memoir, *A Promised Land*:

> *"It was as if my very presence in the White House had triggered a deep-seated panic, a sense that the natural order had been disrupted. Which is exactly what Donald Trump understood when he started peddling assertions that I had not been born in the United States and was thus an illegitimate president. For millions of Americans spooked by a Black man in the White House, he promised an elixir for their racial anxiety."*

Donald J. Trump is the miscegenated incarnation of an unholy gestation and the source of all our fears and uncertainties. He breathes to trigger and cultivate antipathies, demonize his challengers, justify the hatred he exhales with every word he utters. His main tools of governance have been the lie and the blackjack. Repulsive as he may be, Trump is less the source of Amerika's decline than a consequence of its downward spiral. To live under him while in full possession of one's faculties was to be in a perpetual state of rage and despair.

◆

We all surmised that the virus would mutate, behave erratically, assume new monstrous identities, sicken at random, and kill indiscriminately. A pall of sadness, incomprehension, and anxiety would descend upon the land. And, despite their best intentions, epidemiologists were still in the dark about Covid-19. We lived in fear—fear of the raging pandemic, fear of political turmoil in Amerika, fear of a crumbling economy, fear of hysteria, fear of rising crime and civil unrest.

THE *MESSAGE* IS THE MEDIUM—I began putting pen to paper at an early age. It's a technique I first explored in the salacious billets-doux I lobbed at the girls in elementary school when the teacher wasn't looking. Folded origami-like into sailboats, birds, airplanes, and flowers, my overtures produced little more than elfin giggles. I persisted, convinced at the time that a well-turned epistle is the shortest path to a girl's heart. I would soon be transferred to an all-boys' school when the teacher concluded that I was after more than just the heart. Writing took a more serious turn in high school with the encouragement of lustful coeds and a curriculum that entailed written essays on the works of Pascal, Voltaire, and Rousseau, and those of the hypnotic Kafka, whose surreal allegories and two decades-long dialogue with friends, paramours, fellow writers, and editors sheds an eerie light on his fixations.*

We also parsed excerpts from the copious eleven-year conversation between Germany's literary titans, Johann Wolfgang von Goethe and Friedrich Schiller. Their writings survey the metaphysical and esthetic ideas of their era, and advance often divergent views, notably on the French Revolution, an event whose roots and consequences are still the subject of heated debate and which I, a Paris-born anarchist, continue to applaud as it helped purge France of a decadent monarchy, a toadying aristocracy, a venal merchant class, and a depraved clergy. (When it comes to revolutions, no one does them better than France. When the French government dares to turn its back on the people, the people paralyze or set the country on fire. If only the people of Amerika had French balls in their sagging scrotums).

Anyway, the idealist Schiller (1759-1805) asserted that to make use of political freedom, one must first be free. He

---

* In time I came to regard Kafka's bizarre visualizations of existential anxiety as unalloyed realism.

pleaded, to no avail, that King Louis XVI's head be spared. The considerably more pragmatic Goethe (1749-1832) doubted that the masses are capable of political maturity. He did not devote much time to contemplating the circumstances under which such maturity might be nurtured. He believed that men, when galvanized politically, lose perspective of what is essential — truth, integrity, freedom, egalitarianism, justice. Worse, they look away when the common good is being sacrificed at the altar of dogma and partisan politics. This crippling sabotage of the national psyche (I would describe it as the *"breakdown of a nation's cognitive faculties and the dumbing down of its people"*) took on a frightening aspect when Donald J. Trump … a shady entrepreneur, pussy grabber, bully, racist, draft- and tax-dodger, and pathological liar who coddles bloodthirsty despots; who displays open hostility toward women and minorities; who threatens to cut off funding to media outlets he deems *"purveyors of fake news;"* who intimidates journalists he calls *"enemies of the people;"* who pardons convicted criminals in exchange for unconditional loyalty; who encourages crowds of adoring philistines to beat up demonstrators; and who brags that *"nothing would happen"* if he killed someone on Fifth Avenue … became the de facto dictator of the United States of Amerika. In acquitting the impeached president, the most openly corrupt person ever to occupy the White House, the Senate enthroned and anointed a king. His trickeries, lies, scams, malapropisms, jingoism, and overt threats provided an inexhaustible wellspring of dark humor for some journalists while fueling the trance-like admiration of his worshippers, all of whom seem to be missing (or are embarrassed to admit openly) that Trump is not only a diabolically clever con man, but a megalomaniac whose Amerika-on-fire campaign strategy, to work, relied on urban violence to boil over right up until Election Day, and for enough uninformed or willfully blind voters to conclude that it is spiraling into an abyss of anarchy and barbarity … for which he is entirely to blame. Unless ousted and neutralized, everyone knew, he would make bullying, persecution, and revenge the hallmarks of a second-term presidency.

◆

A hundred senators cast judgment on Trump, but the saga of his impeachment would be put to rest when the ultimate jury—150 million voters—delivered a final verdict at the polls. Trump's acquittal was never in doubt. No one expected him to be removed from office as the two articles of impeachment demand (one would have been enough: abuse of power). But these are not normal times. The US, as I characterized it three years ago, had turned into a Mafia state, structurally (with oligarchic layers of power and control as the supreme governing entity), as well as in the character of its immoral conduct and objectives. The *"heartland"* of Amerika spoke through 49 senators not inclined to risk their bread and butter by defecting. Republican Mitt Romney voted his conscience. He has since been showered with invectives and veiled threats by Trump, whose fury and penchant for revenge are well documented.

◆

Am I the only one to detect a palpable degradation in modern society's ability to absorb and process torrents of information, some legitimate, much of it bogus and disseminated in ways calculated to inflict maximum consternation or to reeducate an unsuspecting or befuddled public? Few people can distinguish between real and spurious scientific data, between legitimate political rhetoric and propagandist brainwashing. The Internet is inundating us with an avalanche of half-digested data and *"alternate facts."* Social media, an incessantly gurgling toilet bowl of inanities, offer not a single post that has any resemblance to real knowledge or fact. The Fourth Estate, tasked with separating fact from fiction at an ever-faster tempo, can't keep pace. The brain can no longer simultaneously gather and process information. We either consume it raw, unaware of its irrelevance or toxicity, or we digest it and forget about it like yesterday's bowel movement. Recent research in neurophysiology has confirmed that when exposed to an endless flow of data the centers of our brain responsible for information processing short circuit and rebel. The simplest rules of logic no longer apply. We can no longer distinguish between real, hard-core fact and reptiloid conspiracy theories. Fact is no longer what is recorded but how it is perceived.

LIKE-MINDED ALTER EGOS—If solitude is the self-granted privilege of free men (an essential extravagance in my case) good company is not a given. Like an aromatic and palate-pleasing potage whose confection calls for the meticulous blending of choice ingredients, friendship is born of the serendipitous encounter between compatible doppelgängers who, over time, enable the cultivation and fusing of shared values, outlooks, and objectives. It is no coincidence that the individuals with whom I converse on a nearly daily basis are endowed with engaging personalities and views so very much my own that our camaraderie is as fresh and stimulating now as the day it began—in some cases more than fifty years ago.

Three are fellow Frenchmen. I've known "Luc" since we were kids, when we engaged in peeing contests (who could pee the farthest), short-sheeted the beds of our bunkmates in boarding school, smeared the upper lip of dozing kids with rotting Camembert cheese, and drew unflattering, often obscene, caricatures of the acerbic and shark-toothed math teacher. Recently widowed, a polymath and skilled writer who deplores the cultural decadence of the times, "Luc" lives in a beachfront, ivy-cloaked stone house in Normandy. A stickler for the purity of the *"langue de Molière,"* he watches over my French, dulled by sixty-five years in the US and riddled with what he scornfully calls *"Americanisms."*

"Paul" is a high-ranking political office holder, a socialist, fierce anti-papist and fellow Freemason with a passion for pre-Columbian art and an aversion for the *"Trump-like"* policies and *"spoiled-child conceit"* of French President Emmanuel Macron. He lives alone—*"one day my wife decided she prefers women so she packed her things and left,"* he shrugs—in a rambling country cottage in Gascony, the exquisite pastoral province in southwestern France where D'Artagnan was born and, 270 years later, where my father, a physician and duelist of sorts, joined the Maquis, the guerrilla band of French Resistance units that valiantly fought against the Germans during the Second World War.

"Mathieu" is a Paris-based fine arts dealer and ardent Zionist whose support for Israel and panicky cries about the meteoric rise of anti-Semitism in France do not inspire in him the slightest urge to move to the Land of Milk and Honey. He and his wife live in an upscale neighborhood in a spacious art-cluttered top-floor apartment with an unobstructed view of the City of Light's most iconic landmarks. I share his unease at the rebirth of fascism in France, but his impetuous backing of the apartheid and repressive Netanyahu regime remains a source of polite friction between us. I lived in Israel, later served in its diplomatic corps, and I am mindful that Prime Minister Benyamin Netanyahu and the rabbis who enthroned him have no intention of making peace with the Palestinians. I keep providing him with evidence of Israel's hegemonic ambitions, to which he responds with a mixed bag of contrite rationalizations. A man of refinement and culture, he struggles with the ambiguities of our age. He finds in art and the fortunes he has accumulated a convenient escape from a troubled conscience.

"Keith" — we worked in New York nearly forty years ago — is a tall, soft-spoken, urbane Texan whose gentle ways, mordant wit, and unwavering friendship I cherish. A writer long ripe for retirement who finally got off the *"merry-go-round,"* he deplores Amerika's *"obscene flirt with fascism"* and accuses Evangelical Christians of *"waging war on democracy."* Trump fills him with revulsion:

> *"Refusing to acknowledge defeat, concocting meritless lawsuits that almost certainly will come to nothing ... he may linger on as a force in US politics. He knows that his base will follow like drooling hyenas. This destructive being — an evil child masquerading as an adult — is busy adjusting the firewall that protects his primitive*

ego. The 'transition' to January. 20 is perfect space for someone who had not expected to lose to recalculate, destroy, exact revenge, exude venom, bite, scratch, and enjoy the rabid support of his base. I'm already hearing talk of a run for the White House in 2024, a TV show, perhaps impromptu maskless rallies, and public masturbations that mesmerize his base, encourage rebellion, demonization, all of which are instinctive to disturbed children. At the core, for Trump, politics was never anything more than a means to an end in support of a bottomless, voracious ego which, fantastically, I do not believe 71 million voters ever imagined. That is my definition of insanity."

To stay safe, Keith often seeks refuge from the Lone Star State's blimpish politics in the remote and magnificent Big Bend Park.

Born in Crimea, an alumnus of the KGB's Military Institute of Foreign Languages (he speaks six languages), "Yevgeny" is an incurable globe-trotter now marking time in Croatia after lengthy stints in France, the US, Hungary, and Turkey. He and I also met in New York where we collaborated on a series of research projects. A follower of the *Extinction Rebellion**, he is a vocal critic of *"the tourism apocalypse"* which, he asserts, disfigures the planet. He also riles against the airlines:

"One round-trip flight from New York to London creates a warming effect equivalent to two or three tons of carbon dioxide per person."

He is especially critical of cruise ships:

"One cruise ship emits as much pollution as a million cars and generates about 15 gallons of hazardous chemical waste in a single day. Passengers and crew aboard the biggest ships produce 210,000 gallons of sewage and almost five times as much graywater—from

---

* The Extinction Rebellion is a socio-political movement that uses nonviolent resistance to protest climate breakdown, biodiversity loss, and the risk of human extinction.

sinks, showers, toilets, kitchens, and so on – in a single week. And, in a year, 100 million gallons of petroleum products from cruise ships seep into our oceans."

Yevgeny reserves his bitterest and most alliterative criticism for the *"clusters of clueless Korean 'cruiseniks' who come ashore and take selfies, and the bands of boisterous Bosnian babushkas who pee and defecate in public."*

A frustrated reformer, he produces an on-line newspaper whose contents enrage his mostly Russian subscribers ... or leave them cold. He likes to *"bug"* people but resents the angry, often incoherent feedback his posts inspire. Indifference and neutrality infuriate him. He believes we are too stupid to survive and insists that our *"unfettered mating habits"* endanger the planet. Nothing prevents good science from being ignored like malice and conspiratorial silence. He is willing to bet his last kopek that no one will ever lift a finger to save the world from itself, not even when it sinks into an irreversible coma.

If he has one regret, it's spending a few years in Amerika where, for the first time in his life, he experienced depression. *"It was as if I'd been locked up for no reason."* He still refers to Amerika as *"the Land of the unfree, the Home of the paranoid. When you live in Amerika,"* he told me recently, *"you are bound to be depressed. All intelligent, thinking people I have met there were depressed. Every single one of them. I have met more intelligent people on Prozac in Amerika than anywhere else. Amerika crushed me, turned me into the opposite of what I once was."* He calls humans *"talking apes,"* finds *"mankind's obsession with longevity sheer idiocy,"* and *"clinging to life repulsive."* His nihilism is refreshing.

"Emilio" is an inventor, a former CIA operative with a master's from Yale and a Ph.D. from Cornell. He and I co-founded a successful but short-lived insider's defense/ intelligence quarterly surveying the worldwide proliferation of nuclear, biological, and chemical weapons. *"When I saw Notre*

Dame engulfed in flames," he wrote, "my first thought was of you. I knew this would hit hard." It did. His missives always end with the same counsel: "Stay away from the news. It's disheartening

A native of Punjab, "Gurvinder" is a veteran airline pilot, a Sikh, and one of the serenest human beings I have ever known. We met and became fast friends in southern California when, revolted by the brutal beating of a young Sikh by racist thugs who mistook him for a Muslim [Sikhs grow beards and wear turbans], I visited the local Gurudwara (Sikh Temple) and offered my condolences.

"Bill" is a California-born novelist and gifted painter. He's been living in Honduras for nearly half a century. I befriended him during my twelve-year stint in Central America. Outwardly undaunted by but not oblivious to the poverty, unrelenting violence, and paralyzing corruption that plague this chronically failed state, he reflects stoically on the meaning and consequences of old age, and shuttles regularly between his hilltop studio on the outskirts of Tegucigalpa and the golden north coast beaches of Trujillo.

♦

Eight people, freethinking, well-read, endowed with the kind of intellectual curiosity that promotes scholarly discourse, all sharing the same impatience with ignorance and stupidity, all convinced that humans and their institutions are unprincipled and immune to reform, all atheists but one. The lone exception follows the divinely inspired way-of-life counsel of eleven gurus whose one-size-fits-all version of deity leaves ample room for nonconformist interpretations. My "god," I once told him as we discussed various systems of belief, inspires reverence, not worship, arouses wonder, not fear, needs nurturing, not rituals. Gurvinder smiled impishly. I sensed he was trying to digest my words. "The Gurus would have no problem with that *characterization,"* he said. *"Yes, God and Nature are one and the same."* How refreshing. The same depiction drew angry objections from an Evangelical Christian who called me a blasphemer.

All are men. No woman I know has shown the remotest interest in pursuing a sustained dialogue. It's not that I haven't tried to engage them; I did my best to elicit some reaction to the ideas I advance. Their responses are invariably tardy, monosyllabic, oblique, guarded. They'll gladly keep me on the phone for an hour but will not commit two sentences to paper (or electronic mail). Their caginess triggers memories of my late mother and grandmother, both witty raconteuses, both disciples of the Age of Enlightenment literary salon-style of storytelling made fashionable by Madame de Sévigné and Madame de Staël. The works of these 17th- and 18th-century French noblewomen are still read and enjoyed for their wit, effervescence, and astute portrayals of the hypocrisy, debauchery, and intrigues that plagued the genteel if utterly decadent society of their epoch.

◆

Heeding Freud's counsel that a good rule for exchanging ideas is *"to leave unmentioned what the recipient already knows, and instead tell him something new,"* is not easy. Sometimes I revisit the facts, rehash the obvious, and keep an eye peeled on events that support or invalidate my commentaries or most cautious prognostications.

What follows is a kaleidoscopic meditation on the state of an ever-changing universe straddling such diverse preoccupations as politics, the absurd, and pandemics — the diseases that kill and the virulence of irrationality, the arrogance of blind faith and the humility of uncertainty. Edgy, cynical, defiant, the ensuing omnibus is set down unredacted, which explains the sometimes-irreverent tone or coarse language with which it is liberally spiced. My harvest, a fraction of a near-daily dialogue, would have been dramatically foreshortened had I not cultivated, through the years, a small coterie of ideologically congruent alter egos eager to indulge me as I stew, literally and figuratively in this stifling Swamp, and if the monotony of this green fetid hell had not made such catharsis central to my sanity. Ultimately, the *message* is the medium. The content, not the method by which it is transmitted, is what will stir or scandalize, inspire, or outrage those who go beyond this preamble. My aim was to reveal myself, my thoughts, my feelings, my weaknesses, my biases, and my wants with all the honesty I can muster but without a scintilla of regret or remorse for the perplexity or outrage they might engender. I am not St.-Augustine, and this is not a confession. It's a repudiation, an indictment. No pretense of a remedy for the world's multilayered and intersecting ills discussed in this work is implied, only the sadness, bitterness, and anger they continue to evoke.

NO VACANCY — The Swamp is a place without expectations. I never thought I'd end up in its uninspiring, teeming vastness but you see, every deed, ostensibly freely undertaken, can be traced to an endless succession of decisions, some heedless, others driven by false hope, stupidity or the illusion of free will, and dearly paid for with bitter, everlasting regret.

In the womb there was warm, comforting darkness, silence, serenity. Then I was born in a Paris private clinic where chic ladies have their babies or abort them. I pretested, I'm sure, at this unwelcome expulsion into a reality I had neither foreseen nor would cheerfully welcome. And there followed events over which I had no control, incidents that led to other unexpected, uncontrollable situations to which I grudgingly submitted until I was old enough to take control of my life and whereupon I proceeded to make one bad choice after another.

If you recall, I moved from New York to the southern California desert following the tragic events of September 11, 2001. This estrangement seemed justified at the time, so painful was the spectacle of a gravely wounded and dispirited giant. I remember seeing smoke rising in my rearview mirror as I drove west across the George Washington Bridge. I wept. I had spent most of my adult life in the Big Apple and I had adored the city and hated it at times with the same raging passion and exasperation that had sustained and poisoned some of my liaisons. Leaving New York for the Antelope Valley, which I began to appreciate just as I readied to trade its wide-open spaces, spectacular vistas, eternally blue skies, and technicolor sunsets for the scorching, swarming Swamp, may have been driven by reflex, as it had some forty years earlier, by my equally reckless exodus from France where I was born — not to mention the dozen or so changes of domicile in between.

In late June of 2018 after twenty years in the Golden State, we moved to the Swamp for reasons we are still trying to justify. We should have had our heads examined. Shipping furniture and other belongings by truck, we loaded up our car and left our Mojave Desert home for the broiling, dank, schizophrenic climate, homicidal traffic, and culturally starved bog we now call home. Free will? Actions that seem freely taken or spontaneous may well spring from some distant, primal impulse that only vigilance and common sense could anticipate and help abort. Hard as one might try, it is sometimes impossible not to step in shit. One judges a stupid act, big or small, by the regrets it elicits and the torments it inflicts.

I know. Those who long for the past are not always understood. *"Stop bleating,"* uncharitable souls exclaim. *"The past is gone. Get over it, move on."* Pleading that *"things were better yesterday"* is something an old-timer has earned the right to do, especially if the epoch, the setting, and the existential realities he now faces compare unfavorably with some portions of his past. Certainly, diseases that killed twenty years ago can now be treated or eliminated but the stupefying stresses to which we are now subjected have spawned other maladies, similarly afflictive and often just as fatal. Yes, things were better when we killed each other with clubs, bows and arrows, swords, and muskets instead of assault rifles and nuclear bombs. Yin and yang, complementary symbols of the absurd duality of existence made possible the splitting of the atom and the production of prodigious quantities of energy ... while pushing the world ever closer toward an inexorable holocaust. Such conundrums are legion. For us, yes, it was better in California than in the Swamp—and infinitely better in New York before that. It was better still when cell phones had not yet been invented and when people, young and old, didn't spend hours spellbound, staring at little electronic screens, fondling them, taking selfies, and exchanging twaddle long distance. It was better when people read books, took long walks, paid each other visits, and conversed face-to-face, when the art of letter-writing had not been reduced to a few truncated syllables, when we didn't kill time slumped on a sofa like beached whales in a state of catatonic stupor in front of the TV, and when people actually swam in swimming pools instead of lolling on their noodles or lazing around, vacant-eyed, like hippos in the Serengeti. And it was certainly better for me in France when I was twenty, brimming with vitality and idealism, and when the predictable ravages of old age were still far off. When someone says, *"Things were better then,"* I understand. I don't ask for an explanation. I don't argue. Nostalgia is the ontological birthright of those whose future is now well behind them. Melancholy is a form of sadness felt when remembering what was once and cannot be again.

◆

Anyway, somewhere in the wilds of New Mexico, halfway between Silver City and Deming, along the lunar outcroppings of the City of Rocks, our car overheated, hissed, sputtered, groaned like a wounded beast, and expired. I took this calamity as a providential hint: Let's turn around and head back to the High Desert. But putting in a new motor would have cost more than the car was worth, so we rented a van and resumed our eastward Swamp-bound journey. To save time, we followed the shortest and most scenic route — the southern edges of California, Arizona, New Mexico, Texas, and so on.

Anyone who has driven cross-country will agree that the US is magnificent. One vivid and memorable impression this transcontinental odyssey produced was its sheer size and the vast stretches of barren geography — thousands of square miles of nothingness, from horizon to horizon, from sunup to sundown, uninhabited if spectacular expanses of utter emptiness as far as the eye can see. Gee, we mused as we rolled along Interstate 10 ... there's a lot of vacant space, a lot of room here. Think about that when someone in high places says, *"We're full.*

We have no room. Go home. Go back where you came from. You don't belong."

I would later make the inescapable connection between endless empty space and asylum seekers fleeing chronic droughts, agricultural collapse, endemic poverty, inept governments, and gang violence in a talk I was invited to give at one of the Men's Club's monthly breakfast meetings. Half a dozen people walked out on me muttering obscenities under their breath. *"Commie! Fake news! Enemy of the people!"* The Swamp has its quota of inhospitable critters, but some of its humans are the most offensive. I'm not an enemy of the people. I'm an enemy of demagoguery, bigotry, and hypocrisy.

◆

The immigrant crisis the US faces is also a by-product of global warming driving people from parched areas toward the higher, more prosperous latitudes. Equatorial regions will need to be evacuated during the next 30-40 years. What we are dealing with now are only the early stages of a much larger mass exodus. Very few Norwegians, if any, will ever move to the tropics.

WHAT AM I DOING HERE?—I welcome nature's justifiable wrath. While I do all I can to leave as small a carbon footprint as possible: I drive sparingly, recycle, use canvas bags at the supermarket instead of plastic, abstain from red meat, buy organically grown fruits and vegetables, install low-wattage lightbulbs. I no longer fret over mankind's headlong dash toward self-immolation. Fretting about insoluble problems leads to headaches, ulcers, and depression. I wouldn't deliberately poke myself in the eye; why should I wring my hands, beat my breast, and lament the inevitable? What good does it do scientists to issue alarming warnings that no one heeds, and what do I gain by heeding them when I know both the plot and the no-exit punchline?

What I struggle with is a disheartening and ossifying perception of my fellow man—cannibalistic, greedy, corruptible, violent, hypocritical, apathetic, slothful, and dreadfully stupid. I'm turning into a recluse in my old age—not that I was ever a social butterfly when I was young. Even as a child, and despite my mother's exhortations to go out and play, I chose to stay home. I'd read, draw, spend hours, spellbound, seated cross-legged in front the huge Blaupunkt radio listening to strange languages and exotic music. I'm the guy who stood against a wall at the far end of a living room during a shindig (on those rare occasions when I agreed to show up) observing with annoyance the displays of inane merriment unfolding before me and asking myself, *"What the fuck am I doing here?"* I'm the fellow who buries his head in a book or pretends to be sleeping on a flight, bus or train so I don't have to interact with the passenger sitting next to me. I'm the chap who lets the phone ring if the caller ID reveals the interloper is someone I don't wish to talk to at that moment. I'm the bloke who, at the pool, chooses a spot that's as far away as possible from a crowd of sonorous sunbathers. I've been practicing *"social distancing"* long before this clumsy euphemism was ever coined. Wearing a mask is a routine I no longer resent.

◆

Is it me, or does the Swamp breed (or attract) an unusually large number of unexceptional beings? Is it the sun, the heat, the humidity? Is it the rusting green, the tedium of a landscape over-saturated with dying palm trees? Yes, palm trees are dying at an alarming rate, poisoned by organisms awakened and energized by climate change. Is it the wearisome sameness of a flat, uninspiring topography; the urban sprawl, the latticework of intersecting roads, all impossible to tell apart because they all look alike? It is all these things? Leaving the California desert was an act of sheer folly overshadowed only by our mindless flight from New York in 2001 — an absurdity further dwarfed by my inexplicable emigration from France forty years before that. What am I doing here? Life is a leitmotif.

CRIMSON HELL — We have entered an epoch of unreason and diminishing prospects. We are at once spectators and participants in the absurd tragicomedy that has engulfed the world. Whereas I used to sneer in disgust at the news, I now shrug them off and move on. I no longer expect that people will come to their senses. A grasp of history and man's natural ferocity underscore the futility of hope. Utopia is like a rainbow: you see it, you admire it, but the closer you go towards it, the farther it retreats. There is some comfort and safety in indifference.

◆

The monotony of our existence offers a measure of wellbeing that evaporates the minute we venture outside: Endless traffic. Deafening vehicular noise. Reckless drivers. And the damn shriveling palm trees as far as the eye can see. The Swamp.

◆

I thought I had no tears left. I cried when the Germans occupied Paris (I was three); when my father was arrested by the Gestapo (I was four); I was thirty-six and fifty, respectively, when my mother and my father died, she of pancreatic cancer at the age of fifty-nine, he of congestive heart failure at eighty-three. I cried when John and Robert Kennedy and Martin Luther King and John Lennon were assassinated; when the majestic towers of the World Trade Center collapsed on September 11, 2001. I shed tears of impotence and fury at the sight of hungry, emaciated children wasting away in some desolate, sunbaked, famine-ravaged pueblo while old-moneyed elites and parvenus live in Babylonian opulence. I cried when twelve people were murdered during the attack on the satirical *Charlie Hebdo* newspaper offices in Paris in January 2015 — eight journalists, two police officers, a caretaker, and a visitor--and yet again ten months later when one hundred and twenty-eight people were mowed down in coordinated terrorist attacks in various parts of the City of Light. Other random acts of incomprehensible brutality against innocent victims in the US and elsewhere — more recently New Zealand and Sri Lanka — keep shocking me to my core.

I weep now, heartbroken and dumbfounded by the tragic spectacle (reminiscent of Jerome Bosch's crimson visions of hell) of Notre Dame de Paris Cathedral going up in flames. For me and for all those who know its history and marvel at its splendor, Notre Dame embodies and symbolizes the genesis, the heart, the very soul of the city of my birth. Indeed, it was on the small island on the Seine from which it rises that Paris (first known as Parisii, named after the Celtic Iron Age tribe that founded it, later as the Roman encampment of Lutetia) was born. I can't believe what my eyes were forced to see. It's as if a part of me was being incinerated. And when the cameras panned briefly downward from the burning spire onto the square below, I saw Parisians, fellow Frenchmen, and visitors from around the world fortunate enough to have gazed at its iconic façade and marveled at the treasures it holds under its arches and in its alcoves — also weep as these terrible images unfolded.

Coined in medieval times and emblazoned in Latin on its coat of arms, Paris' motto is *"Fluctuat nec mergitur"* — rocked by the waves but never sunk. It will take years, decades, but Notre Dame, we are told, will be rebuilt, revived. Of course, what was forever consumed, including pseudo-relics, will sadden aesthetes and the faithful alike. The loss of the carpentry work is infinitely more tragic — nine centuries of history irremediably reduced to dust in a few hours. Having endured the ravages of time and witnessed man's aberrant acts of violence, Notre Dame de Paris will continue to epitomize the spirit of my beautiful two-thousand-year-old hometown. But I can't quite yet erase from my mind's eyes the crimson flames that engulfed it.

MONEY ÜBER ALLES — Donald J. Trump may be an imbecile — he often acts like one (or like a cranky kindergartener) — but make no mistake: He's a clever and diabolical con artist whose malevolent antics and incompetent governance are shamefully ignored or loudly applauded by those he purports to champion.

The only reason he disbanded the advisory committee* is that it only had one member from *"industry"* and that its detractors, all from industry (or profiting therefrom) ignominiously portrayed it as a "Socialist" ploy. Trump received millions in financial support from private donors and large corporations, most of them global-warming doubters whose interests he promoted and from whose revenues he may continue to profit long after he leaves the White House.

◆

An article in *The Nation* warns that the proliferation of plastics will lead to a worldwide ecological catastrophe. In response, US companies are investing $65 billion to expand plastics production, arguing that *"the challenge is not with plastics themselves; it's what happens after people use them...!"** The counterargument that the problem is tied to the very existence of plastics falls on deaf ears. When it comes to money, reason and scruples fly out the window. I'm waiting for tobacco companies to say, *"There's nothing wrong with cigarettes ... if you don't inhale"* and the liquor industry to argue that *"one cannot turn into an alcoholic unless one imbibes ..."*

Meanwhile, hard as it tries, the US can't (or won't) envisage what an alternate energy future might look like because it's so

---

* The Trump administration disbanded a 15-person advisory committee that helped communicate scientific climate change findings to businesses and government officials.

** Or as the National Rifle Association likes to put it, *"Guns don't kill people, people kill people...."*

accustomed to and dependent on the existing multi-billion-dollar fossil-fuel economy. Solar, wind, geothermal, hydropower, and conservation all work. But opponents say, *"There's no money."* Baloney. The US is drowning in money. The problem is that it's in the wrong pockets and that it's being spent on the wrong *"priorities."* Nearly 1.5 million US troops and mercenaries are currently deployed in eighty countries—nearly half the planet! No wonder Russia, Iran, China, and North Korea are hardening their arsenals.

DEATH AND TRANSFIGURATION—What I hear about Mamula Island, whose existence was unknown to me, is outrageous but not surprising.* Time marches on, survivors die, memories fade, and greed takes over. It is not farfetched to predict that recent expressions of man's inhumanity to man will be studied and viewed by future generations with the same detachment as the Hun invasion of the west, the Golden Hordes of Genghis Khan, the Crusades, the *"Holy"* Inquisition, the calamitous Conquista, the Armenian genocide, Shoah, the Hutu-Tutsi bloodbath. More blood would since be spilled and more will be shed. Even the First and Second World Wars, and the Korean and Vietnam debacles are fading from memory as new conflicts arise. The average teenager knows little, if anything, about the Holocaust. Apathy feeds ignorance—and vice-versa. It will take a while before Auschwitz, as some sardonically suggest, is turned into a five-star resort, but there will come a time when this chamber of horrors is neither remembered nor lamented.

The Earth is a self-regenerating graveyard. If you drive the breadth of the US you will cross hamlets, towns, and mega cities built on the sacred grounds and bones of millions of Native tribes that were slaughtered by *"frontiersmen"* – thugs wearing raccoon hats and wielding Bowie knives who elbowed their way westward—and whose decimated remnants live in poverty in their own land.

◆

---

* Currently uninhabited, the island of Mamula is known for its chilling history as a WW II concentration camp. Wedged between Montenegro and Croatia in the Adriatic Sea, it is home to an abandoned fort that was once used by the Italian army to incarcerate, torture, and execute prisoners. The Montenegrin government recently approved a proposal to transfigure this grim stone relic into a luxury resort.

From antiquity to modern times, successive civilizations built their empires on the ruins of their predecessors. Temple Mount was part of the ancient Jewish shrine in Jerusalem. Muslims built a mosque over it. The Great Mosque in Istanbul was built on the site of the palace of the Byzantine emperors, in front of the basilica Hagia Sophia, which was a Greek Orthodox holy place. It is being turned back into a mosque. The Romans built over the graves of more than half of western Europe, the Middle East, and northern Africa. They were overtaken by the Visigoths and Ostrogoths. I too abhor the idea that a former torture chamber might be turned into a resort. The senior retirement community where we live (1,000 apartments, a club house, two swimming pools, tennis courts, and two artificial lakes into which domestic waste is discharged) was erected on land once inhabited by ancient native American tribes.

When night descends, I can hear the mournful sobs of a thousand ghosts.

TWIN THREATS—Trump and his cronies may not accept the scientific reality of climate change, but senior US military and intelligence officers, I am told, acknowledge that global warming and concomitant climate disturbances are causing extreme droughts and torrential monsoon rains, crop failures, mass migrations, and civil unrest, and they are devising emergency measures to prevent these phenomena from spiraling into nuclear war. They warn that soaring temperatures, melting polar ice caps, and rising sea levels will impact food and water supplies in resource-poor areas prone to civil strife, thus increasing the risk of starvation and widespread violence. As Professor of Peace and World Security Studies, Michael T. Klare, argued warily in the conditional tense in the January 27, 2020 edition of *The Nation*:

> *"In a world constantly poised for nuclear war while facing widespread state decay from climate disruption, these twin threats would intermingle and intensify each other. Climate-related resource stresses and disputes could increase the level of global discord and the risk of nuclear escalation; the nuclear arms race would poison relations between states and make a global energy transition impossible."*

Forty years earlier, in his epic bestseller, *Cosmos*, astronomer Carl Sagan pondered:

> *"Are we willing to tolerate ignorance and complacency in matters that affect the entire human family? Do we value short-term advantages above the welfare of the Earth? Or will we think on longer time scales, with concern for our children and our grandchildren, to understand and protect the complex life-support systems of our planet? The Earth is a tiny and fragile world. It needs to be cherished."*

Fifteen years later, in his chilling *The Demon-Haunted World: Science as a Candle in the Dark*, he added:

"Science is more than a body of knowledge; it is a way of thinking. I have a foreboding of an America in my children's or grandchildren's time – when the United States is a service and information economy; when nearly all the key manufacturing industries have slipped away to other countries; when awesome technological powers are in the hands of a very few, and no one representing the public interest can even grasp the issues; when the people have lost the ability to set their own agendas or knowledgeably question those in authority; when, clutching our crystals and nervously consulting our horoscopes, our critical faculties in decline, unable to distinguish between what feels good and what's true, we slide, almost without noticing, back into superstition and darkness."

A chilling commentary on the principle and effects of causation. Today's talking heads keep speculating. One gets a sense of the confluence of their individual assumptions but no clear vision of a specific end-game scenario. It may not matter. The US military deployed a new submarine-launched low-yield nuclear weapon, something the Pentagon sees as critical to countering Russia's arsenal of smaller tactical nukes and which several former high-ranking administration officials warned would increase the potential for a nuclear conflict. The Navy may also arm a new destroyer with a conventional missile capable of hitting any target on earth in one hour. How comforting.

A THANKLESS PROFESSION — *"No one likes the bearer of bad news,"* wrote Sophocles in his play, *Antigone*, in 441 BC. Journalism is the first draft of history and journalists are often the first to be sacrificed in its name. While revisionists busily trivialize the truth, falsify it, bury it, slander those who pursue it, muzzle them and, in extremis, liquidate them, journalists capture the images, the sounds, the imperishable smells of the human drama. We are accused of telling unseemly truths, of seeking the *"bête noire,"* of ridiculing high-ranking scoundrels, of lamenting illegal, immoral, and unwinnable wars. Sometimes we're even accused of treason. Our embarrassing, often troublesome, always inappropriate disclosures are methodically anathematized by those they target. We are the purveyors of *"fake news,"* the *"enemies of the people."*

When our reports irritate or madden our leaders, we are accused of giving the public palpitations. We are even blamed for the pervasive profligacy that society, to endure it, prefers to forget. Everything we say is microscopically, maliciously scrutinized and dissected as if our writings concealed some subversive coded message. Some of our fiercest detractors even advocate censorship. They demand that the press look elsewhere or be silent. They are so shaken by the truth that they want to repeal it, erase it, cremate it. History is full of auto-da-fes in which bearers of bad news are immolated.

This may explain why some journalists, to survive, turn away from the onerous questions of the day and look at the lurid miscellany that the public hungers for. Some fixate on the daily banalities that take us away from the cold hard facts. Others applaud the demagogues and regurgitate the enormities they spew. In the process, they disgrace themselves professionally by misinforming the public. *"Political correctness"* (the sacrifice of truth at the altar of hypocrisy) appeases readers and placates advertisers who care only about revenue.

Our mission is to look for, discover, and disseminate facts. We do not get paid to solve the evils we unveil. Exposing ugly truths is not an act of treason. Criticizing is not unpatriotic. It is the right and duty of every citizen. A free and independent press is the backbone of democracy. The real traitor is silence. To remain silent is to conspire.

OF PANGOLINs, BATS, AND SNAKES — Not so very long ago I was wondering what calamity would wipe out humanity: The Great Extinction (currently underway) or a nuclear inferno (not to be discounted). Then, lo and behold, a satanic, crown-shaped, ruby-speckled microbe said to have been spawned in some putrid Asian *"wet"* food market where live poultry, fish, reptiles, and mammals are caged helter-skelter in sickening intimacy, mutated, jumped from animal host to unwary human guest and thwarted my most pessimistic omens. Its advent is being blamed on the fiendish crossbreeding between a pangolin, a bat, and maybe even a snake, a frivolous speculation that does not explain its genesis — the repeated rape by man of his home planet, and the ongoing destruction of the natural habitats of the animals he blames for his self-inflicted woes.

◆

Early on, a vile stench wafted over the deserted streets of Amerika's cities, the exhalation of the lungs of a dying monster. Capitalism was in a state of cardiac arrest. The super-rich risked losing their fortunes — while the poor were losing their jobs, their healthcare insurance, their homes, and their lives. From this time forward, I ventured, the history of humankind will be inscribed in two chapters: pre-coronavirus and post-coronavirus.

Thousands of people continue to test positive for the virus. Thousands have died. Thousands more will expire. Nations around the world, on advice of medical experts, have imposed varying periods and modes of *"social distancing"* and *"self-quarantine."* Of course, neither the pangolin, the bat, nor the snake is at fault. The guilty party in all this is man who destroyed these creatures' habitats and enabled this lethal hybridization.

So long as the crisis lingers, people will wring their hands, pound their chests, indulge in tearful sentimentality — or rebel. They will forget everything once the crisis subsides or an effective vaccine is created and go right back on doing what they did before — feast, party, give life to children who do not ask to be born in the wretched world that their parents bequeathed, vote idiots into office, lie, cheat, steal, make war, and pretend that they somehow hold a special place in a universe contemptuous of their existence. *"Normal"* is what, in time, people get used to ... until a new crisis comes along to distract them from their unexceptional existence. Sadly, stupidly, these same people are convinced that when their planet dies of exhaustion (it is already in a sad state of affairs) a fresh one will be provided ... which they will proceed to pillage and desecrate with typical nonchalance. It is unwise to suggest that humans are capable of learning from their mistakes.

Scientists and health experts are all warning that it's only the beginning. Meanwhile, we have a president, a narcissist and right-wing demagogue who emboldens unhinged anti-Semites and domestic terrorists, who insults journalists who dare ask inconvenient questions, a pathological liar and a sociopath who cares little about the scourge that continues to sicken and kill thousands of people every day. People have taken to hoarding. Fearing shortages and civil unrest, they are arming themselves. The sale of weapons is growing across the land. And as if they had nothing better to do, today's gurus — the ever-loquacious bloggers — suggest that the coronavirus is a Chinese biological weapon launched against the West. We have a very large number of imbeciles ready to believe (and disseminate) what conspiracy theorists are spinning in order to spread panic, to create ever wider political divisions, perhaps even to encourage martial law in order to facilitate the advent of a fascist dictatorship and a second Trump mandate. Amerika, the presumptive "leader of the free world" is hopelessly adrift.

Covid-19? A wakeup call, one of many we have blatantly ignored.

A SELF-DEVOURING HYDRA—Journalists arm themselves with words. Their adversaries—a triumvirate of collusive self-interests—wield an arsenal pointed at the truth: Those who pretend to manage the world's economy by imposing an elitist and fictitious *"New Order"* at the top; those who aim to foster and maintain profitable colonial empires in the middle; and, well at the bottom of these vampiric structures, the docile regimes of debtor nations that salivate like Pavlov's dogs when their creditors ring the bell of foreign aid. Journalists hope their words endure. They do, for a while, on the printed page, but they are soon forgotten. Or they leave behind them a muddle of rhetoric that however eloquent or poignant does little to temper human nature, tame passions, rein in hatred and prejudice, and stop violence. Neither Nietzsche's assertion that *"God is dead,"* nor the sarcasms of Lucian of Samosata or the assertive atheism of Rabelais, Kafka, Camus, Sartre, Rushdie, and Dawkins have succeeded in distracting men from their obsessions any more than the Ten Commandments have the power to eliminate evil. Some illusions and some horrors are beyond words. Pogroms, exile, torture, war, ethnocide. All have been swept aside in a tide of uninterrupted human suffering. The shocking images aired on prime time of man's inhumanity to man do not lie. The world, news bulletins tell us, is a cloaca in which we wade, knee-deep, in the blood of martyrs. At the dinner table, we see them dying or fading away like phantoms. Our fragile, overworked psyche forces us to gloss over history—the Crusades; the *"Holy"* Inquisition; the Conquista; the extermination of Amerika's native peoples; slavery; the massacre of more than a million Armenians; the Holocaust; Biafra; the killing fields of Cambodia; the inter-tribal carnage between Hutus and Tutsis; the bloodbaths in Chiapas and the jungles of Guatemala; the recurring spasms of violence that pit Israelis and Palestinians; the wars in Iraq, Syria, and Afghanistan; the murder of street children by agents of the state in Central America. I could go on.

◆

Geography, ethnic differences, cultural incongruities all encourage us to intellectualize other people's agonies. We endure their pain by erasing from our minds the images that such atrocities conjure. *"You can't change human nature,"* we pontificate as we partake of dessert. In a pinch, an inane sitcom will put us at ease. We survive reality by looking the other way. We have honed the art of killing and the savage beast we are roars with increasing ferocity. The human race is a hydra whose sole purpose is to multiply and, when the time comes, to devour itself. This is all an immense, comical, heartbreaking, sordid, dreadful performance, a carnival where jugglers, conjurers, tightrope walkers, contortionists, and freaks reign supreme.

A CASE OF FUTURE PAST—The trick is not to panic. Even pandemics run their course. Vigilance and basic precautions should help ride the crest of this tsunamic wave. We are, as much as possible, curtailing all unnecessary outings and avoiding unnecessary contact with people. Yesterday we stocked up on food and water. Our reserves should last at least two weeks. And we wash our hands several times a day, something we've been routinely doing for years. For the rest it's karma.

According to an online conspiracy theory, author Dean Koontz is said to have divined the coronavirus outbreak in 1981. His novel, *The Eyes of Darkness* mentions a killer virus called "Wuhan-400"—eerily predicting the Chinese city where Covid-19 is alleged to have surfaced. But the similarities end there. Wuhan-400 is described as having a 100-percent *"kill rate,"* and alleged to have been developed in labs outside the city as an incurable biological weapon. Covid-19 has a kill rate of about two percent. An account with more similarities, also credited by some as predicting the coronavirus, is found in the 2011 film *Contagion*, about a global pandemic that jumps from animals to humans and spreads randomly around the globe.

Remember *The Andromeda Strain*?

It is not uncommon for writers to anticipate the future. Jules Verne (1828-1905), the father of science fiction, predicted interplanetary travel, the nuclear submarine (Nautilus), glass skyscrapers, high-speed trains, gas-powered automobiles, computers, elevators, and worldwide communications at a time when such ideas were considered fantasy.

Written in 1863 but first published one hundred and thirty-one years later (1994), *Paris in the Twentieth Century* follows a young man who struggles unsuccessfully to live in a technologically advanced, but culturally backwards and morally defunct world. Often referred to as Verne's *"lost novel,"* the work paints a grim, dystopian view of a future civilization poisoned by technology. And long before Verne, Leonardo da Vinci (1452-1519) drew plans for the helicopter, the parachute, the anemometer, the diving suit, the armored car. Sometimes imagination and coincidence trump prophecy.

It is interesting to note that the predictions made by the Bible's apocalyptic prophets (Ezekiel, Habakkuk, Daniel, Hosea, Isaiah, Jeremiah, Micah, and John) can be said to have come true. They were lamenting the decadence of their epoch; they knew that past is prologue. In fact, they were picturing and decrying the present in which they lived.

◆

I don't know what is worse, Covid-19 or Trump but their conjunction was catastrophic for Amerika. The pandemic will ease or end at some point but if Trump prevails, whatever is left of democracy in this country will be gone. As he speaks, the totalitarian noose is tightening around our necks. It is not farfetched to envision the end of press freedom, curtailment of free speech, gulags, and *"reeducation centers"* — concentration camps where minds are robotized, subverted or *"turned off."* I cannot help but be amazed and, yes, horrified, that the man is still in office and that other than a few brave journalists and maverick lawmakers no one is saying anything that might galvanize the citizenry to recognize in this 21st-century Caligula the monster he really is.

IF ONLY—If only the US had implemented a policy of social distancing a week earlier, it could have prevented more than half of the number of coronavirus infections and deaths. And if only the country had locked itself in two weeks earlier, it could have prevented 84 percent of deaths and 82 percent of contagions.

Although hints of an impending disaster were detected in November 2019, the first US case was not reported until late January 2020. It was not until mid-March that the Trump administration, reluctantly following the recommendations of the Center for Disease Control and Prevention, encouraged people to avoid crowds and limit their movements. It was also at this time that cities like New York decided to close their schools.

Epidemiological modelling to assess transmission rates from March 15 to May 3 helped determine the impact that social distancing could have. The first few days were decisive. During the initial growth of a pandemic, infections increase exponentially. Therefore, early intervention and rapid response are essential, researchers said. But they admitted that they could not explain how people would have responded to previous policies:

"Public compliance with the rules of social distancing may also be lagging behind due to a suboptimal awareness of the risk of infection."

At this writing, the 50 states are somehow *"open."* If local leaders detect a growth in new cases, they will have to respond quickly. Delays will result in a stronger rebound in infections and deaths—an exhortation that does not seem to have been heard by the thousands of rebels who, to claim their *"rights,"* do not hesitate to sacrifice the health, even the lives, of others. One must conclude, sadly, that little or nothing will be done to effectively and decisively delay or cancel the inevitable toll of a pandemic of which little is yet known. Unlike animals, humans are the only creatures who put themselves in the unenviable position of having to solve self-created problems that they could have avoided had they not stuck their heads in the sand.

CRETINS, KILLERS, & KLEPTOCRATS — Social scientists tend to view human history as an evolution from bestiality to cultural refinement. Chroniclers of the here-and-now, journalists are less sanguine. In the aggregate, our accounts demonstrate that human society seesaws wildly between states of stagnancy, feverish creativity, uneasiness, chaos, unbridled violence, and all-out war. While these oscillations can be blamed on history's cretins, killers, and kleptocrats, they are hastened, prolonged, and fossilized by public torpor and a disdain for democracy also known as fascism.

Educated, painfully shy, ill at ease with court life and hopelessly disconnected from the masses, France's King Louis XVI was, by all accounts, a cretin. A ruler who spends his time tinkering with clocks, tending his rose garden, and chatting with *"God"* must be a cretin. So was czar Nicholas, a spineless party-going autocrat who played dominoes, munched on caviar and ladyfingers, and drank champagne while his people starved and his wife made goo-goo eyes at the sinister Rasputin.

In contrast, Hitler, Stalin, Mao, Pol Pot, the Shah of Iran, Ceausescu, and Saddam Hussein were killers. So was Cuba's Fulgencio Batista and his ideological cousins, Chile's Augusto Pinochet, Guatemalan generals Romeo Lucas García, and Efrain Rios Montt, Honduras's Gustavo Alvarez, and Peru's Alberto Fujimori. They all resorted to premeditated murder — indiscriminate or selective — as a means of wresting control and ensuring blind submission from the people. And, as the people passively danced to their executioners' song, inertia, fed by fear, helped prolong the suffering.

Kleptocrats, a term that aptly describes several African, Asian, and Latin American heads of state — and at least one US president — specialize in purloining net wealth from commoners and transferring it to the upper classes into which they were born (or into which they aspire to ascend). Some kleptocrats have also been cretins and/or killers; Honduran army chief, Luis Alonzo Discua Elvir, a CIA asset and death-squad leader, comes to mind: a bullheaded halfwit murderer. Another archetype kleptocrat (he stole millions of dollars from the Fondo Petrolero) was Honduran President Rafael Leonardo Callejas. In Honduras, a kleptocrat's success is measured by just how large a percentage of the tribute he extracts from the people is retained and enjoyed by the elite.

◆

Despite assertions that most Hondurans embrace an egalitarian system of governance, Honduras remains a fractured democracy. It is one thing to espouse an ideology on paper. It's quite another to put it to work. While social scientists wrestle with statistical abstractions and theoretical models, we journalists working in the field have long since diagnosed the problem with overt but seemingly fruitless candor. On an empty stomach, democracy is an empty slogan. Democracy does not work in a vacuum. People must vigorously take part in the process. Failure to do so further empowers cretins, kleptocrats, and killers to exclude the people from the process.

I ask, what is the difference between a poor 18th century Frenchman and an indigent 21st century Honduran as far as life and expectations are concerned? What traits distinguish a relatively small band of Frenchmen—derelicts, vagrants, beggars, and petty thieves armed with pikes, scythes, and cleavers who managed to overthrow a hated monarchy—from the vast Honduran masses who continue to get screwed by successive dynasties of corrupt, inept, and apathetic regimes? What will it take to awaken the masses? What will bring them to their senses, lead them to the streets, and give them the courage to demand justice? The answer lies in how they rationalize their misery. The fact that a kleptocrat is still in power and that another cretin/killer/kleptocrat will most likely take over speaks volumes about the moral fiber of the citizenry and explains their unceasing torment.

MYTH AND PARANOIA—In an editorial published in the *Connecticut Post* in August 1997, I called for Israeli Prime Minister Netanyahu's resignation. Describing his policies as *"myopic, truculent, and regressive,"* I condemned the expansion of settlements in occupied areas of Palestine and petitioned for an immediate and permanent cessation to the expropriation of Arab lands, a practice rebuked by the international community and seen as a blatant invitation to unrest and violence.

I also denounced dastardly alliances with jingoist generals and scandalous covenants with religious zealots in Brooklyn and Jerusalem designed to force a theocracy on a largely secular society. I questioned the Likud Party's inexplicable compulsion to scuttle peace negotiations, its wrathful scorn of world censure, and its long-standing and savage antipathy toward the Palestinian people—all hallmarks of an administration oscillating between gaucheness and aberration—and posing grave danger to peace and stability in the Middle East.

In short, Mr. Netanyahu's regime, I asserted, was a calamity and a recipe for disaster. Roundly denounced, my views would be validated by ensuing events. Mr. Netanyahu's stern governance brought not one iota of security—perceived or actual. Instead, as successive political crises between his administration and the Palestinian National Authority deepened, Jews and Arabs found themselves mired in frustration and endless conflict. Mr. Netanyahu's combative style and pugnacious rhetoric exhumed and revived old hatreds, reopened festering wounds, and triggered a new swell of cynicism, misgivings, and suspicion.

Israelis are demoralized; some are disgusted, others are terrified. Israel's friends are exasperated, her enemies galvanized, former negotiating partners are livid. Bitterness and rancor deepen with every stroke of Mr. Netanyahu's ministerial pen, every hostile decree, every calculated vacillation, every broken word, every rubber bullet fired at stone-throwing youths.

This pernicious alchemy, formulated in the name of *"national security,"* has yielded confusion, anxiety, sorrow and, yes, insecurity. Heartened by the short-lived prospects of a peaceful resolution of their protracted dispute, Israelis and Palestinians now teeter between bewilderment and apprehension, defiance, and bloody paybacks. Neither side can endure the suspense and agony of military occupation. Spasms of punitive violence have since nullified erratic and snail-paced steps toward peace.

Last, I warned that myth, paranoia, and blind chauvinism had hopelessly tainted Mr. Netanyahu's alleged vision of peace and security. Twenty-five bloodstained years later, Mr. Netanyahu, who was reelected to an unprecedented fifth term amid charges of bribery and fraud, is pushing Israel on a new collision course with the Palestinians and its steadfast and forbearing US ally. Betraying his ghoulish patriotism, his intransigence, and lifelong hostility toward Palestinians (he considers them *"a sinister and divisive element,"*) have invigorated the religious Right, whose enormous financial resources continue to underwrite his campaigns and whose gluttonous territorial expansionist objectives he has obsequiously bowed to. His recent oratory, including bombastic threats of annexation, rule out any chance of a modus vivendi. Issued from the sword and resting on some of the Bible's less than endearing exhortations, his policies have daunted attempts to bring about stability and peace.

Given these sobering realities, one might infer that Mr. Netanyahu, his titanic ambitions fulfilled, and his acolytes placated, never intended to make peace in the first place. His actions and words suggest that his administration, from the beginning, was bent on breaking the spirit of the Palestinian people. Hard line begets harder line. Security by intimidation, repression, and economic persecution feeds animosity and results in insecurity. He who sows the wind reaps the tempest.

As I write this, I am painfully reminded of what the hawkish Gideon Sa'ar, former minister of the interior (and a past information chief at Israel's Consulate General in New York, where I worked for a time as a press officer) said at a staff briefing on the prospects of peace. To this day, I cannot say whether Sa'ar was stating policy or relishing a moment of wishful thinking*:

> *"It is not in Israel's strategic interests to make peace with the Palestinians. To insure Israel's hard-fought hegemony, we have no choice but to weaken the resolve of Palestinians by attrition, provocation, psychological warfare, the expropriation and colonization of occupied parcels of land and, ultimately, the absorption of Palestinians into a one-nation Jewish state."*

This astounding declaration prompted my early resignation from the consulate. I had also begun to recognize that diplomacy (politics/propaganda/deceit) and journalism are perilously incompatible … if not mutually exclusive. Israel's subsequent stance and deeds seem to confirm Sa'ar's prophetic avowals. Meanwhile, as the Palestinians, outnumbered, marginalized, strangers in their own land, are struggling to preserve fragments of their shrinking patrimony, new synagogues are rising on confiscated land.

---

* Sa'ar is said to be Netanyahu's most likely successor.

SWAMP FEVER—Meteorologists in the Swamp get it wrong nine times out of ten—summer and winter. To their credit, they predict past weather events with uncanny precision and sometimes sheepishly admit that divining the weather *"in these parts is tricky."* They never apologize when they're wrong. The weather we are having is atypical for this time of year. It should be clear, sunny, mild, and dry. Instead, we haven't seen the sun in a month: It's raining, and the humidity level is reminiscent of Calcutta under the monsoon. Science blames global warming, global dimming, and an increase in aberrant, often violent phenomena that meteorologists strangely and doggedly refuse to characterize as abnormal or even unusual.

I continue to follow the *"Extinction"* debate in the world press and in various science journals. I recently called the local TV station weather desk and asked why meteorologists never mention global warming and climate change in their forecasts or analyses of atypical conditions. No one would take my call. I suppose mentioning these trends would be poison for the network and might get the meteorologists fired. No one wants to be the bearer of bad news. I think I said that somewhere else.

Meanwhile, friends in France report gale-force winds, torrential rains, and destructive floods … while California and Colorado are ablaze, bone-dry Australia is on fire, koalas, wombats, and kangaroos are dying by the thousands, and a huge typhoon is bearing down on the Philippines.

IRREVERSIBLE CESSATION OF LIFE—Language is a wondrous and mighty tool. Power over words means power over ideas and power over ideas translates into power over people. The government has considerable influence on our thoughts in the way it wields its power through language. One method often carried to its fiendish extremes is *"doublespeak,"* an ornate and allegorical idiom crafted to disguise the actual meaning of things and most often used by government, the military, and businesses to dupe the credulous, the ignorant, and the uninformed. Some of the figurative lingo coined by do-gooders (or tricksters)—terms like *"animal companion"* (pet); *"challenged"* (handicapped); *"wardrobe malfunction"* (runaway nipple); and *"downsizing"* (mass firings)—evoke smiles, compassion, or exasperation. Others, like *"correctional facility"* (prison); *"economically disadvantaged"* (poor); *"post-traumatic stress disorder"* (shell shock); and *"ethnic cleansing"* (genocide) arouse scorn.

These deceptions are called euphemisms. In his visionary novel, *1984*, George Orwell dubbed them *"newspeak"* and *"doublethink,"* fashionable composite nouns,

> *"deliberately constructed for political purposes: words which not only have a political implication but are intended to impose a desirable mental attitude upon those using them."*

Take the US Army's short-lived oxymoronic recruitment slogan, *"Army of One,"* or the equally inane *"Be All You Can Be"* (can one ever be more than one already is?), later changed to the bombastic *"Army Strong."* Designed to galvanize gung-ho superpatriots, these moronic slogans gloss over the fact that soldiering means unquestioned obedience to authority and unavoidable risks that include death.*

---

* And who can forget Melania Trump's pompous and illiterate, *"Be Best"*?

Doublespeak is most reminiscent of Orwell's cautionary tale when it is articulated to cover up some unpleasantness, something that has negative connotations for large segments of the public and which, say, a government agency is forced to coin to avoid backlash by replacing a term with a new one that most people will not recognize as signifying the same thing. Thus, *"area denial munitions"* means landmines. *"Extraordinary rendition,"* stands for the illegal kidnapping of enemy combatants who are then handed over to the authorities of another country for grilling. *"Alternate interrogation techniques"* is doublespeak for torture. *"Operational fatigue"* is the current version of PTSD. *"Collateral damage"* describes the wartime mass slaughter of civilians. *"Suspected terrorist hideout"* refers to any civilian home destroyed by US troops whether terrorists hid there or not. *"Asymmetrical warfare"* translates into any effective combat tactic not taught in war college. *"Self-injurious behavior incident"* alludes to attempted suicide. And, decoded, *"USA-Patriot Act,"* signifies Uniting and Strengthening Amerika by Providing Appropriate Tools Required to Intercept and Obstruct Terrorist Acts—a decree rammed through without debate, plebiscite or national referendum even though it deals a devastating blow to civil liberties while granting the government unlimited powers and virtually no oversight.*

◆

If the foregoing mumbo-jumbo were not enough to set off a collective wave of nausea, consider that, a while back, a key government report on malnourishment eliminated the word *hunger* to describe a persistent condition afflicting nearly 15 percent of US households. People lacking the funds to buy food, families in which parents skip meals so their children can eat,

---

* The USA-Patriot Act was later *"hardened"* by a program dubbed "Total Information Awareness" which, once stripped of its pseudo-techno veneer, means spying on the citizenry without probable cause.

and seniors who must choose between dinner and life-saving medicines are now grotesquely categorized as having *"very low food security."* In other words, some 35 million people who rely on soup kitchens and other charity for daily sustenance are not necessarily hungry; they just don't know where their next meal will come from. *"Food insecurity"* is an obscene term calculated to ease the collective conscience while artfully underplaying what amounts to a national tragedy and a disgrace. Last, eradicating poverty in Amerika is done through *"gentrification,"* the process by which the character of an impoverished urban area is changed by rich people moving in and displacing the poor inhabitants in the process.

◆

Given my age, kicking the bucket, giving up the ghost, breathing my last, biting the dust, meeting my maker, crossing the Jordan, croaking, falling off my perch, hopping on the last train to glory, passing away, pulling up daisies, and going to my eternal rest is a *"foregone conclusion"* (fated). I can see it already: My demise, with characteristic ceremonial absurdity, will be attributed to an *"irreversible cessation of life."* So much for euphemisms.

BEING HATED: A TRIUMPH OF SORTS—How to explain some of the negative feedback I receive from uninformed skeptics or, quite likely, from the purveyors of misinformation and master propagandists who get paid to influence public opinion by denying fact or contradicting any opinion that might inspire an anti-establishment backlash?

For about five years (2002-2007) I wrote a weekly column on a variety of subjects. Scrupulously erected on a scaffold of verifiable fact and enhanced with commentary, the column ran both in the print and online editions of a regional California daily newspaper. While the editor picked among the contentious letters he chose to run as proof of the paper's impartiality, he was less discriminating with the bloggers who engaged in vicious attacks against anything that did not agree with the publisher's version of reality. I was routinely the target of nasty verbal assaults. I later discovered that some of the agents provocateurs were paid by the publisher to counter any opinion that might offend some readers or, worse, displease his precious advertisers. Others were government *"plants"* whose job is to monitor the media and screen reader feedback.

It is no secret that we are being surveilled in Amerika—what we buy, eat, read, listen to on the radio and watch on TV; what medicines we take; what organizations we join, who we vote for. Our landline telephones are routinely tapped; the GPS in our smart phones and cars reveals (and presumably transmits) our location—even when not in use! To discourage or prevent intrusion I blocked the eye of the camera on my PC ... just in case. You can no longer trust anyone because everything you do in this skittish, schizophrenic country is subject to scrutiny. The trick in a nation of superficial freedoms and crumbling values is to avoid raising suspicion. Going too far with our denunciations could be costly. I continue to pay the price.

♦

I don't write to please readers, enlighten them, make them see things the way they really are. The closer I get to the truth, the farther they retreat. I keep going, not because I'm likely to change the world but because what I say, I hope, will survive, on paper, in cyberspace, or in the memories of those I challenge. Somewhere, somehow, what I say will strike a chord with someone who is liable to alter the course of history. Unorthodox ideas, unfathomable truths eventually electrify people and spur them to world-altering action. All great ideas meet resistance at first, but they leave indelible traces that often trigger intellectual revolutions. I do not have to win over a thousand people. Touching one or two will suffice. Writing dystopias, as I have learned from bitter experience, does not win popularity contests. All things considered, being hated for championing a good cause, for telling myth-killing truths, for stirring something in my readers' fear-paralyzed psyches is a victory of sorts. Being ignored is what I fear.

THE MORE THINGS CHANGE—I made a career of galling people. Very short-lived accolades by a trifling number of fellow travelers aside, my polemics have been met with resentful indifference, vitriol, and, in two instances, death threats. I spent twelve years in the belly of the beast (Central America), unmasking vampires and pushing for reforms that would help improve the lives of oppressed ethnic minorities. Twelve years. Upshot: *Nada!* As witnessed by the desperate asylum seekers' struggles to escape poverty and gang violence, and find refuge in the US, things are now much, much worse. The unrest in parts of Central America explains the continuing exodus from its shantytowns and impoverished villages. I will not have the indelicacy of asking why anyone would want to live there. I too would have absconded from these irredeemably failed states a long time ago. What I witnessed and experienced on my last foray, in 2006, was a bitter foretaste of things to come. Fifteen years later, the more things change ... the more they stay the same, but at a higher pitch, with increased violence and no prospect of an equitable resolution. When a handful of venal and incompetent dynastic families own and control everything in sight—the media, banks, utilities, and transit system; when the constabulary, lawyers, and magistrates can be bought, when garbage piles up on roadways and city sidewalks, when the healthcare system is near the bottom in world rankings (after Russia, Peru and Guyana), and when the average *"querido ciudadano"* is in constant fear for his life, I say, get on the *Bestia,* hombre, join the exodus, and chance it *al norte.**

---

* El tren de la muerte (The Death Train) refers to a network of Mexican freight trains that US-bound migrants ride to traverse the length of Mexico. It is also known as La Bestia (The Beast) and El tren de los Desconocidos (The train of the unknown).

ARGUMENT FROM WEAK ANALOGY—I've been debating whether I should ignore the tepid response my article on Israeli expansionism elicited or offer a measured postscript. I opted to say nothing. I fear that the ethical questions the article raises have eluded a core of Jewish readers. Most were livid. Others retreated to a neutral corner by using an argument from weak analogy, *i.e.*, that if things are similar in some respects, they are perforce analogous in others. In other words, they speculated, perhaps with calculated malice that Israel's *"Palestinian Problem"* is intractable ... so why bother? Doing so spares them the effort of taking the high road. Blaming intractability for sixty-plus years of harsh Israeli military occupation, the dehumanization of the Palestinian people, the theft or bulldozing of their homes and orchards, the expropriation of their ancestral lands, and the increasing erosion of their civil rights is a diversion—and an evasion—not a stance. Last, instead of condemning injustice, they are legitimizing Gideon Sa'ar's jingoist pronouncements and, in so doing, trivializing the outrage, pain, and anguish I expressed in my original article. Being a Jew and feeling an emotional, albeit nebulous, bond with Israel, does not prevent me from recognizing despotism.

No one is disputing Israel's right, nay, the obligation, to protect against those who would threaten its existence. But as the undisputed victor and iron-fisted occupier, should it not also show some chivalry and compassion toward the vanquished? Not all Palestinians are terrorists. Instead, Israel's rabbinical stranglehold on an apartheid regime has made a mockery of the Golden Rule: *"You shall not take vengeance or bear a grudge, but you shall love your neighbor as yourself."* Worse, it vilifies the very document that represented the first public expression of support for Zionism by a major political power and which sowed the seeds of Israel's future founding, namely the Balfour Declaration, which states:

"His Majesty's government view with favor the establishment in Palestine of a national home for the Jewish people, and will use their best endeavors to facilitate the achievement of this object, it being clearly understood that nothing shall be done which may prejudice the civil and religious rights of existing non-Jewish communities in Palestine, or the rights and political status enjoyed by Jews in any other country."

Have Jews, after millennia of persecution, exodus, dispersal, and near extermination, forgotten what it is like to be second-class citizens? Or are they reenacting the very horrors that led, spurious speculations contend, to the erection of a new nation on the usurped bedrock of an existing one? Had they accepted to make their home in Uganda, would they have subjugated its tribes, stolen their lands, burned their homes, and ghettoized them under military rule?*

Is the urge to avenge their ghastly past so irresistible that they are willing to commit the same crimes that earned them, for a time, the world's empathy? The suggestion that criticism of Israel is anti-Semitic (I have been accused by imbeciles of being a *"self-hating Jew"*) is a canard peddled by people whose selective memory has deprived them of a conscience. I am a Holocaust survivor; such insinuation is nauseating.

---

* At the Sixth Zionist Congress at Basel on August 26, 1903, Theodor Herzl proposed British Uganda as a temporary refuge for Jews. Other countries under consideration included Iraq, the Dominican Republic, Canada, and Australia. All were eventually rejected in favor of a national home in Palestine.

SILENCE IS GOLDEN—I was recently told I am suffering from a *"social anxiety syndrome,"* a simplistic and inaccurate rendering by a lazy or unimaginative physician of a lifelong incompatibility with people—especially crowds—not an irrational fear of them. It's an allergy, not a mental illness. I never understood why people congregate and gravitate around each other. On the contrary, I consider the herd instinct, this compulsion to throng together, to be a disorder. An abhorrence of shared communal norms may not win me a popularity contest, but I never aspired to be popular. I might come off as antisocial, a cantankerous old weirdo enamored of solitude, but nuts, I'm not.

Adding insult to injury, I also suffer from hyperacusis, a malady defined as a highly debilitating hearing disorder characterized by an increased sensitivity to certain frequencies and volume ranges of sound. Experiencing sensory overload, a person with severe hyperacusis has difficulty enduring everyday sounds, which become painful or irritating.

As one can imagine, the two conditions make life difficult. Leaving the house exposes me to sounds that raise my blood pressure and heighten my discomfort. I avoid restaurants; people bark at each other instead of chatting discreetly. A trip to the supermarket makes me ill. I find relief only when I get back home. If I were in the slightest religious, I would concur with the contemplative monk who once told me, *"Silence is God's abode."*

◆

Went to the pool, did my twenty laps (1,500 ft.) No sooner out of the water than the sky turned black from horizon to horizon and the fireworks began. It rained violently for a good thirty minutes, horizontally at times. Palm fronds were being ripped from their trunks and deck chairs were flying about. I had to take refuge inside the clubhouse as blinding lightning strikes and deafening thunder filled the air. This is as close as I've been to a hurricane. I suspect the real thing is far worse, perhaps a legitimate reason to abscond, soon I hope, from this fusty Turkish bath.

"The Swamp is a dump," warned "Yevgeny" when, after ten years, he tired of living on his boat on some brackish lagoon and moved back to Europe.

"If you're not a complete dysfunctional moron you will not fit in. The people in the Swamp are not nice. They are superficial, rude, racist, and narcissistic. With the lack of education, low wages, months of unbearable heat and humidity, it's easy to understand why everyone is so miserable. I can't imagine why anyone would want to live in this fen. It's an idiot's paradise."

I should have listened. I have reluctantly made peace with the idea that we are, at least for the time being, stuck here.

CROSSING THE LINE — There's much even my most intimate friends don't know about me (not because I keep secrets but because some aspects of my life never came up in conversation). Likewise, I probably don't know everything about them. In time, however, we may divulge (or discover) things heretofore unrevealed ... like me getting laid on a Greyhound bus en route from New York to Pittsburgh or being fellated on a redeye from New York to Los Angeles — I think it was a Pan Am Clipper — or deflowering a young Mary Baker Eddy disciple in a lifeboat on a transatlantic crossing in exchange for my solemn vow to embrace Christian Science.

Nor do I think I ever fully chronicled my early times in New York. One day, the mighty Herald Tribune, where I'd worked as a copy boy sharpening pencils and running errands, expired, the victim of a series of disastrous business decisions, and aggressive competition from The New York Times. In a few years, in rapid succession, New York, Amerika's media capital, went from a dozen dailies to fewer than a handful. The war for jobs, fierce and bloody, proved beyond my capacity to wage. I was now twenty-two, inexperienced, quixotic, naïve, and ill-equipped to compete in an industry where natural selection produces its own tiger sharks.

Survival dictated that I set aside any serious journalistic aspirations, and there began a slow, steep ascent consisting of one unsteady step forward and three breakneck backward slides. I went to work for *"trade"* publications in the food, beverage, plumbing, medical, and aviation fields. My longest job — I took over the reins of an environmental sciences magazine when the editor could no longer hold his liquor — lasted eight years. I attribute this extraordinary longevity to daring, luck, necessity in the face of looming indigence, and the esteem of an editorial crew in whose eyes I could do no wrong. Other jobs came and went. I was fired, demoted, laid off. Several publications died under me in rapid succession. Many more moved out of town and were never heard of again. I called myself a journalist but paying rent and feeding a young family demanded that between frequent sorties to the unemployment office I also accept work as a dishwasher, waiter, barman, elevator operator, cab driver, night-shift cable dispatcher, shipping line clerk, insurance underwriter, foot messenger, busboy, and security guard. I remember ferrying books from Columbia University's dank and dusty basement to the main reading hall. I quit after a day or two. I was then hired to manage the Bizarre, a dismal Greenwich Village coffee shop serving unpalatable potions and bad poetry artlessly recited by haggard bards bombed out of their skulls. Some jobs lasted less than a month, many less than a week. I'd be canned for indolence, ineptitude or insubordination, or I'd just quit, reporting for work in the morning, hating the job, and failing to show up after lunch.

I survived and kept writing feverishly, often in anger and frustration, sometimes the docile medium of inspiration, often the instrument of a dull but providential freelance assignment. Neither my accumulated failures nor the friendly if exasperating advice — *"Come to your senses, boy, it's time you learned a real trade"* — sapped my resolve. I was writing and getting better, if not yet good enough, at what I did best.

Sometimes, in exchange for quasi-security, one is forced to give up one's freedom and swallow one's pride. The New York Academy of Sciences, where I worked as a copy editor, fostered a climate that bordered on sadism. Mrs. Eunice Thomas Miner, the executive director, was an ogress. Diminutive, capable of glacial stares and pinched-lip sarcasm, she ruled by fear and intimidation. Headed by Frank Furness, a meek and unremarkable man past retirement age who trembled in her presence, the editorial staff was recruited from a flotsam of misfits, closeted gay aspiring writers, educated Blacks willing to earn slave wages in exchange for a prestigious Upper East Side office address, and, like me, starry-eyed would-be journalists as yet unprepared to face the dog-eat-dog Fourth Estate. I have no recollection of the texts I edited. I remember working in a Dickensian ambiance where dress and deportment were subject to scrutiny and disparagement, where chatting was forbidden, overtime obligatory, lateness and absenteeism punishable by docking, and a very public tongue lashing compliments of Mrs. Miner followed by a lecture on the virtues of punctuality, decorum, and loyalty in the face of abuse. I quit after less than three months.

Over the years, I would try my hand at many more odd or trivial occupations, all of which I was pitifully unsuited for. My first big break came when I was forty-eight. Years of crushing monotony dissolved instantly in an avenging sigh of victory.

I have since been navigating the murky waters of a nation that uses the power of the press to sabotage democratic norms, to misinform, disinform, and fill the national debate with racist-filled lies and ethnocentric dreck while calling it news. I react by exercising the only form of journalism I know, the kind that rips at society's self-hypnosis and collective superstitions. People always invoke freedom of speech until they hear something they don't like. When people complain that I cross the line, I point out that I didn't draw the line, they did.

♦

Survival in Amerika also dictated that I become quickly acquainted with the salient personality traits that characterize its denizens. Seen from an indelible European perspective, the products of Amerika's mythmaking history:

- Believe without reservation in the fictional image the nation has of itself—a paragon of virtue, incorruptible, selfless, munificent, altruistic, the New Zion, the Promised Land, the eternal glory of *"God"* that the rest of the world must emulate (or else).

- Are obsessed with form but utterly disdainful of substance.

- Will overtake you as you observe the speed limit just so they can get ahead of you even though they have no rational reason to go faster except to reassert their questionable sense of self.

- Will buy an inferior Detroit-built automobile named the Cherokee, the Avenger, the Wrangler, the Taurus, the Explorer, the Cougar, the Falcon, the Mustang, but will not be caught dead driving an indestructible, 24-carat gold vehicle called the Pussycat, the Wimp, or the Fairy.

- Deify sports figures, most of them mediocre human beings who but for their height, brawn, or dexterity with a ball, club, stick, or boxing gloves would be draining your septic tank.

- Self-righteously denounce abortion but cheer when a condemned man is hanged, roasted on the electric chair, or injected with a lethal cocktail of drugs.

- Simulate puritanism and wallow in scarlet promiscuity.

- Are convinced, without tangible evidence, that the rest of the world is unfit to live in.

- Are enamored with and fixated on superlatives—big cars, huge trucks, enormous televisions, mammoth meals, gigantic cereal boxes, gargantuan pizzas. They live in a realm where the biggest, the strongest, the mightiest, the most principled people on earth congregate.

- Are encoded to believe that the two-party system, both tied to corporate wealth, both intent on blocking reform in the name of capitalism, both involved in immense larceny against the poor, is the sole guarantor of democracy.

- Take social studies in school, are taught social graces, are influenced by Social Darwinism, claw their way up the social ladder and, having reached to top, hire social secretaries who handle social calendars brimming with social obligations. Overly sociable, some come down with social diseases. All eventually become eligible for Social Security. Somehow, no one takes umbrage at the word *"social"* except when twinned with the word *"medicine"* which, Great Zeus, suddenly transmutes into some ungodly obscenity, a *"communist"* anti-Christ in the flesh.

- Are enamored of weapons (the bigger, the louder, the more destructive, the better) which, when they're not busy killing each other, they use to hunt because, presumably, there are no supermarkets in Amerika.

- Worship pecs, abs, biceps, and glute's but recoil in horror at the prospect of being perceived as educated, articulate, urbane, and refined.

- Extol the virtues of their Revolution but put down all other insurrections mounted against injustice, military occupation, and persecution as sinister stalinist plots.

- Will elect a moron or immoral president and fiercely defend him so as not to betray their own imbecility.

- Want to spread *"democracy"* around the world and, if need be, will invade, pillage, torture, and kill to impose a commodity they are loath to cultivate at home.

- Recently discovered that Amerika can easily overthrow or liquidate the legitimately elected president of a foreign country but that it has a hard time unseating its own presidential miscreation.

TRAGIC CONTRADICTIONS—Let's keep things in perspective. Jews have been saying, *"Next year in Jerusalem,"* the final prayer crowning the Passover seder, for 2,000 years. Zionism, the movement that spearheaded the re-establishment of a Jewish homeland in the territory defined as the historic Land of Israel (Canaan), was born in the late 19th century. It took another half a century, the rise of Nazism, and the Holocaust to sway the largely recalcitrant Diaspora Jews to the idea of a *"Jewish abode."* Then in 1948 a new nation was created in a territory where very few Jews lived at the time, and the colonization began. You can imagine the Palestinians' dismay, alarm, then fury—they'd been living there for centuries—when they found themselves slowly outnumbered, displaced, expelled, then socially marginalized by people with whom they had little in common (ethnicity, faith, culture, language and political aspirations). Then, as Gideon Sa'ar declared during a briefing about Israel's long-standing blueprint, the ostracism, the ghettoizing, the persecution, the attrition, the psychological warfare, the systematic expropriation and/or destruction of Palestinian homes and lands began.* These actions, condemned by the world community, continue to this day. And people are surprised that Palestinians resent Israel? It's not resentment. It's worse. It's despair. Wouldn't I feel despair if I were in their shoes? I'm looking for some intellectual balance here, some moral equivalence in a quagmire of tragic contradictions.

The Likud Party's hawkish propaganda machine notwithstanding, a huge number of Israelis are mortified. Many are working to reach some modus vivendi with their Palestinians neighbors through joint social, economic, and cultural ventures—members of my family in a Tel Aviv suburb included. No one really believes that Palestinians are committed to *"wipe Israel off the map"* or that they are even capable of such

---

* See page 60

ambitious scheme. That too is a worn canard retold by Netanyahu and his accomplices to keep the embers of fear (and hatred) alive. Everybody knows that most Palestinians are not terrorists. They just want to live in peace like everybody else.

◆

It is no secret that Saddam Hussein was a bad dude but so long as he was *"Our Man in Baghdad,"* the US feted him and subsidized his killing sprees. Same with former CIA asset, Manuel Noriega of Panama. Same with Osama bin Laden, groomed by Amerika and serving Amerika's interests in Afghanistan when the Afghans were fighting the Russians. Same with Chile's Pinochet, Cuba's Batista, the Dominican Republic's Trujillo, and some thirty other criminals the US coddled. Ditto with Hitler, when isolationist Amerika was focused on the Great Depression, not on the rise of a newly hatched monster. It is human nature to condone and justify the crimes of our friends. I shall not be seduced by such dastardly mindset.

Netanyahu's vision of *"peace"* is premised on exclusionary and repressive religious models of citizenship and nationality. His obstinacy forces him to mutilate fact to make a colossal lie more palatable in defense of a nation that is neither democratic nor graced with empathy but rather, as Joshua Leifer, a writer for *Jewish Currents* asserts, is:

> *"… a country that has codified discrimination against roughly 20 percent of its citizens and that for more than half a century has imposed a brutal military regime on millions of people…. A Zionist state cannot be both democratic and Jewish if it guarantees differential rights and privileges based on ethnoreligious identity, [if it] denies basic rights to millions of people and carries out policies according to the racist logic of 'demographic threat.'"*

◆

My article created a tidal wave of ugly, snarling hostility that caused sorrow not shock, rage not embarrassment. I felt as if scourged and crucified by my own people for appealing to their sense of justice and compassion. I heard myself whispering, *"Eloi, Eloi, lama sabachtani?"** Then I remembered that the poignant supplication had fallen on Eloi's deaf ears the first time he heard it, and six million times after that.

---

* "My God, my God, why hast thou forsaken me?"

GOD: "I MAKE HOUSE CALLS"—Declaring houses of worship "essential" during the coronavirus pandemic, President Donald J. Trump, who has never set foot in a church (except to get married), ordered the governors of the fifty states—or else—to reopen houses of worship. He threatened to *"replace"* governors if their states refused to obey his *"recommendations."* It is not clear what specific presidential authority the commander-in-chief was invoking. If I am not mistaken, a recommendation is optional and subject to approval.

"Some governors saw fit to open liquor outlets and abortion clinics, but they abandoned our churches. It's a disgrace. People want to be in their churches," Trump whined at a White House news conference in May 2020. He stopped short of saying that *"God"* plays *"God,"* at will, with or without spectators.

Large gatherings, including those in houses of worship, have led to a rise in Covid-19-related infections and deaths. Two churches in Northern California linked the spread of the coronavirus between church members and clergy during a Mother's Day service. A Texas church later canceled its Masses after the death of one of its priests, and five others were later tested positive for the coronavirus.

During a private interview and under the guise of anonymity, wearing a mask, *"God,"* omnipresent, easy-going, and ready to play the roles that men gave him (or her), said: *"I make house calls. The faithful will find me in the comfort and intimacy of their homes. This is not the time to tempt the devil. Stay where you are. Wear a mask. I'm on duty 24/7 and I'm on my way."*

◆

And lo and behold, in a 5-4 ruling, the US Supreme Court sided with religious organizations in a dispute over Covid-19 restrictions put in place in November 2020 by New York Governor Andrew Cuomo limiting the number of people attending religious services. The case is the latest pitting religious groups against city and state officials seeking to stop the spread of Covid-19, and it underscores the truncheon-like impact of newly enthroned Justice Amy Coney Barrett on the high court. The verdict comes as coronavirus cases are exploding across the country. Predictably, Barrett sided with her conservative colleagues in the dispute as they blithely ignored the expert judgment and warnings of health officials about the environments in which a deadly virus, now infecting a million Americans each week, spreads most easily. Instead of being in favor of public health and savings lives, the Supreme Court surrendered to naïve appeals to *"personal freedom."*

AMERIKA'S BORDELLO — The ever-vindictive, eager-to-be-despised President Trump's ban on travel to Cuba was an act of infantile churlishness. He justified it by claiming that the island nation plays a destabilizing role in the Western Hemisphere, and provides a *"communist"* foothold in the region by fomenting instability, undermining the rule of law, and suppressing democratic processes.

Mr. Trump declined to respond to charges that the US continues to destabilize the Third World by encouraging a fascist foothold and propping up dictators in Australia, Austria, Belarus, Brazil, Hungary, Israel, Russia, Saudi Arabia, and Sweden, and by fomenting insecurity and suppressing democratic processes in developing countries.

And when presidential contender, Senator Bernie Sanders, casually but justifiably praised Fidel Castro's literacy initiatives, Mr. Trump, who worships Putin, Orban, Erdogan, and Bolsonaro, pounced on the Vermont lawmaker, accusing him of deifying a dictator and promoting *"communism."*

Whoa! President Fulgencio Batista, the man Castro unseated, was a dictator under whose governance horrific human rights violations were committed against the Cuban people. Batista, *"our man in Cuba,"* suspended the 1940 Constitution and revoked most political liberties, including the right to strike.* He then aligned with the wealthiest landowners who operated the largest sugar plantations and presided over a stagnating economy that widened the gap between Cuba's rich and poor. Eventually, most of the sugar industry was in US hands, and foreigners owned 70 percent of the arable land.

---

* Franco was "our man" in Spain; the Shah, in Iran; Pinochet in Chile; Duvalier in Haiti; Saddam in Iraq; Marcos, in the Philippines; Trujillo in the Dominican Republic; Noriega in Panama — all in bed with the CIA. And while he fought the Russians, Usama bin Laden was our man in Afghanistan.

Batista's repressive government then began to profit from the exploitation of Cuba's commercial interests by negotiating lucrative relationships with both the States-side Mafia, which controlled the drug, gambling, and prostitution rackets in Havana, and with large US-based multinational companies that were awarded lucrative contracts. To quell the growing discontent among the populace — displayed through frequent student riots and demonstrations — Batista established tighter censorship of the media, while also utilizing his *Bureau for the Repression of Communist Activities* (secret police) to carry out wide-scale violence, torture, and public executions.

The long-awaited and since petulantly rescinded rapprochement between Cuba and the US had been heartily applauded. Friendship and cooperation are always preferable to enmity, isolation, and distrust, especially in an epoch of worldwide turmoil and volatility. Should things improve with Biden in the White House, I hope the good people of Cuba will restrict their association with the US to those trade and cultural transactions that are of clear benefit to Cubans, that do not compromise the sovereignty of their nation, and that do not imperil the Revolution. Cubans old enough to look back to the dark days of the Batista dictatorship will remember that Cuba, at the time, was a Mafia political puppet and Amerika's whorehouse. It would be a great tragedy if normalization of relations between the two countries resulted in the economic buyout of Cuba by US capitalist interests ... and organized crime. Such takeover would inevitably bring back the corruptive influences and misdeeds that precipitated the downfall of Cuba's economy in the 1950s. While I cannot hide my displeasure at some of Cuba's Stalin-style inequities and aberrations, I salute its brave and forbearing citizens.

♦

I am reminded that, as in other celebrated cases (*i.e.*, Panama's Manuel Noriega) it is quite possible that Viktor Bout's criminal activities benefited certain people in the US and that his arrest and long incarceration were intended to prevent him from spilling the beans.* It has also been suggested, not without merit, that if the same standards were applied to everyone, all American gun shop owners *"who are selling arms that end up killing people"* would be in prison.

---

* Viktor Anatolyevich Bout is a Russian arms dealer. Nicknamed the Merchant of Death, he was arrested in Thailand in 2008 on terrorism charges and extradited to the US. In November 2011, he was convicted by a jury in a Manhattan federal court of conspiring to kill US citizens and officials, delivering anti-aircraft missiles and giving aid to a terrorist organization. He is serving a 25-year sentence.

THE GREAT DYING REDUX—Hold on to your breeches. We're about to replicate the Permian Extinction event (or the Great Dying) but on fast forward. In fact, as we speak, the build-up of carbon dioxide in the atmosphere is increasing faster than it did during the extinction that took place 248 million years ago. This has been confirmed by scientific research. The history of the Great Dying offers striking similarities with our current situation. The Permian extinction started with severe jet stream disruptions and the appearance of dead zones in the oceans. This is what we see today. Then, as carbon dioxide levels increased, forest fires became the new norm and Pangaea, the as-yet unseparated supercontinent, was ablaze. Research in the Czech Republic and Italy carried out about ten years ago confirms that massive forest fires were taking place prior to the extinction. Then methane emissions soared, sending temperatures even higher. Ocean acidity rose steeply.

Conditions preceding the Great Dying were strikingly predictive of what we experience today. The planet's mechanism for life extinction hasn't changed. It is more than likely that the future will replicate the past. The next anticipated phenomena include massive methane injections into the atmosphere from thawing permafrost. This is how our planet gets rid of unwanted parasites. This will be followed by hydrogen sulfide emissions from comatose oceans. This is what killed most life forms during the Permian Extinction. Once oxygen levels in the ocean drop and most life forms go extinct an anaerobic decomposition process will produce astronomical amounts of hydrogen sulfide, a gas lethal for all complex biological organisms on this planet.

◆

Just a day before the longest government shutdown in US history, President Trump issued an executive order that called for a 30 percent increase in logging on public lands. The decision was disingenuously billed as *"wildfire prevention,"* though environmental groups say it ignores the role climate change plays in igniting wildfires. Then Trump dropped climate change from a list of national security threats. The decision to delist climate change from national security threats means less Department of Defense research funding and a hostile rejection of the potential impacts of wildfires, droughts, hurricanes, and other natural disasters on planet Earth.

The size and influence of the Environmental Protection Agency shrank under the Trump administration, and so has its prosecuting power. Criminal prosecutions are at a thirty-year low, and many crimes that would have been prosecuted in the past against habitual polluters are now being plea-bargained. The administration says this is streamlining its work, but environmentalists have warned it will lead to more pollution and a faster track to the anticipated Extinction.

CALL IT SCRUPLES—I should have said something when the incident that prompts its belated airing took place. I have been haunted by its urgency for more than five decades. Some fifty years ago as I browsed in a Times Square novelty shop in New York, a young man asked if I needed help. I thanked him and said no, not at the moment. I detected a familiar accent and asked him where he was from.

"Palestine."

"There is no such place," I blurted out. I had uttered these incredibly stupid and humiliating words without a hint of animosity or ulterior motive, the way one talks about the weather. I knew better. I had lived in Israel as a boy and several of the kids I played with in Jerusalem's Greek Colony were Palestinians. My first girlfriend, Leila, a Palestinian, was my age. She was beautiful, smart, refined, and proud. Her father was a respected community leader in a nearby Arab village—Abu Gosh if I recall. My parents, urbane and tolerant, took an instant liking to Leila. Neither said nor did anything to discourage what was my first teen romance.

Our neighbors were not quite as fair-minded. Devious and irresolute at first, the community's resentment toward my parents, first for sending me to a Catholic French school (going to a Hebrew public school would have set me back several grades) reached a furious pitch when I befriended Leila.

One day, a delegation—half a dozen men led by a rabbi—came to our door unannounced, uninvited. The rabbi scolded my father for sending me to a Catholic school and demanded that I be discouraged from *"fraternizing with the enemy."* He meant Leila and my other Palestinian playmates. My father, a physician, and a man of unimpeachable integrity never to be trifled with, especially by bigoted busybodies, stood his ground. He was magnificent. I don't remember his words and won't attempt to reconstruct them for fear of diluting what must surely have been a knockout punch. What I vividly recall is that he opened the door and invited the *"delegation"* to *"get the fuck out."*

Predictably, my father's uncompromising stance did not help mend fences. Acrimony and ugly rhetoric festered for the duration of our tenancy in Jerusalem. Leila ceased to visit. I looked for her. Her father said she was no longer allowed to see me. *"It's best this way,"* he sighed. There was sadness in his voice. I was heartbroken. He had the same look of mortification that I saw in the young salesman's eyes a decade later in New York where I now lived.

It didn't take long to realize the ugliness of my gaffe. I may have uttered a historical fact: There never was a *state* called Palestine but in so saying, I had offended a human being, trivialized his national identity, and stripped him of the things stateless people aspire: nationhood, security, respect, and self-determination.

Time, personal and professional preoccupations dulled the memory of my unforgivable affront. But they did not erase it. It kept resurfacing like a festering abscess, and every time it did, fresh pangs of conscience filled me with regret and remorse. Regret and remorse turned to outrage following President Trump's capricious, despotic, ill-advised, and, for the Palestinians, demoralizing decision to declare Jerusalem the capital of Israel.

I am 83 and retired. I will not dwell on the partisan politics that continue to cleave the Middle East. I will not linger on Israel's hegemonic objectives that doggedly impede the prospects for peace in a land bloodied by decades of violence and acrimony. I have family in Israel, and I wish that nation well. But in the name of decency and justice, as a man, a Jew, a Holocaust survivor, and a veteran journalist, I cannot silently watch the marginalization and, yes, dehumanization of a people who have just as much right to selfhood and dignity and peace as do Israelis. Call it scruples.

Jerusalem is no more the capital of Israel than it is the exclusive domain of Christendom or Islam. It has become the epicenter and bloodstained symbol of the discord and hatreds that only politics, dogmatism, and religious fanaticism can spawn. Palestine exists, in body and soul. I hope the Palestinian people find it in their hearts to forgive me. To all, I say As-salaam alaykum.

FLIGHT OF THE SNOW VULTURES—My friends' ability to distance themselves from the daily media circus is enviable. I am in turn nauseated, alarmed, and incensed by the torrent of insanity and evil I see on the airwaves and in the virtual reality world in which we live. As I watch from a safe distance, I am struck by the notion that a civilization's very magnitude could lead to its demise, that societies are hardwired for self-destruction. They travel an arc from embryo to chronic stagnancy or greatness to terminal decay and collapse. History's graveyard is filled with the cadavers of mighty empires turned to dust, victims of zealotry, arrogance, greed, and moral rot. To avoid the common fate of past civilizations will require a radical change in ethos—the conscious renunciation to the claim of greatness and exceptionalism—lest we hasten a dark age in which the trappings and adornments of civilization are partially or completely lost. A change in ethos, however, is unlikely. Blame materialism, ego, and vanity. That's the macro picture.

At the micro level (I live in a *"senior"* condo complex that encourages fellowship and participation in meaningless activities designed to inspire a fictional communal spirit), I note the same avaricious tendencies, now sharpened by old age, the same narcissism, the same ugly, self-serving politics, the same propensity by small minds scorched by the sun and shrunken by heat and humidity to hold on to trivial but inflexible beliefs with vacuous and ferocious self-importance. I remember old men hunched over a chess board in New York's Gramercy Park and Washington Square. Here they quibble, talk over each other, gesticulate, bark. Only the truth evades them.

As for the Swamp, it's already uninhabitable, with a temperamental climate being the least of its undesirable attributes. Friday was my wife's birthday (it's on February 29 but this is not a leap year, so we threw all caution to the wind and celebrated it on March 1st. We drove to the beach for lunch.

It took nearly an hour to travel eight miles in the company of homicidal drivers who fail to maintain safe distances, go through red lights, tailgate, abruptly change lanes, and cut in front just inches away from disaster. Anyway, *Branigan's* was full. There was a one-hour waiting time for a menu that the best consumer reviews call *"uninspiring beach food."* We wound up at another Irish-named emporium which was also nearly full. The noise was deafening but I held fast. I didn't want to upset my wife who takes my carping to heart, so I said nothing. Of course, there was no way she and I could carry on a conversation. Drowned out, dejected, we just glanced at each every so often between tentative bites of tasteless fare just to make sure one of us had not fled the scene screaming in horror, and jumped in the murky, shark-infested surf. Then I lost it. I asked an especially loud group of seniors seated at the next table—the men were barking, and the women were laughing like hyenas—to please keep it down.

"We have the right to talk."

"You do, but we have the right not to hear you. You're depriving us of that right."

"In public you forfeit that right."

"Nonsense. It's when you're in public that you must be on your best behavior—respectful of others, discreet, demure." I tried reason. "In the privacy of home, you can do whatever you want: Run around in the nude, talk on the phone for three hours, get laid on the grand piano, fart, jerk off, piss in the kitchen sink, and...."

The exchange went nowhere. Social intercourse should foster self-consciousness and a concern for how one is perceived by others. Some people have a hard time controlling their loutish ways. They are cursed with an irrepressible urge to talk. They suffer from logorrhea.* When challenged they fight back. One of the barkers accused me of being antisocial. The others riddled me with dirty looks. And the barking resumed.

By the time we left I was so dizzy from the din and the heat that I nearly passed out. Swamp people don't have intimate conversations in restaurants — they holler. I feel sorry for the waiters and waitresses.

◆

The "beach" was narrow, littered, crowded with merrymaking sunworshippers armed with boomboxes, coolers, smart-phones, and screeching kids. A regular abattoir. We took a walk on the pier, an uninspiring trek during which I was shat upon by a pelican (or was it a pterodactyl?). Perhaps things will improve a bit when the fucking snow-vultures head back north, or when, discretion being the better part of valor, we settle for a cucumber sandwich at home with the shades drawn and Debussy's *Claire de Lune* lilting in the background.

---

* Diarrhea of the mouth.

SKEWED PRIORITIES — The *"upheaval"* is underway and past upheavals provide few lessons on how the current societal cataclysm will evolve. Past is prologue but the dynamics that link past and future are not uniform. While there is a link between cause and effect, not every cause produces the same effect. I'm no scientist but instinct, age, and a fair understanding of history suggest that the future cannot be accurately predicted because intervening chance events occurring between prediction and actualization can and will alter the anticipated results. The consequences of these results follow a similar path of uncertainty. Although Werner Heisenberg (1901-1976) was dealing with quantum mechanics when he formulated his *Uncertainty Principle*, he may have been conscious of its applicability to human events.*

I find it absurd that some social scientists are now busy devising a formulaic barometer of human behavior when so many humans are homeless, oppressed, starving, and dying, when pollution is dimming and poisoning the planet, and when even the once most prosperous societies are showing signs of erosion, fragmentation, and looming collapse.

Human behavior need not be predicted. It is in full view.

---

* The principle that the momentum and position of a particle cannot both be precisely determined at the same time.

BILLIONS OF SEPULCHERS — There was a time when we were children, when life was forever, and fear of the future was an obscure adult preoccupation. Times have changed and today's youth are much smarter and acutely aware of the fatal consequences of an increasingly chaotic world. They are not singing or asking for a less cruel future, they are demonstrably angry, marching in cities around the world, and loudly demanding swift and tangible action against the looming disaster ... while the adults are paralyzed by cynicism, indifference or indecision.

We may be doomed but I can't help but be moved by the poignant appeals and desperate actions of the young, and sickened by the cowardice of the parents who gave them life. Then I look at all the great and mighty empires that rose and fell and the pattern becomes increasingly clear: Self-immolation is in our genes. Barring a sudden, miraculous awakening and intellectual rejuvenation ... we're royally screwed, and we deserve the contempt that our children and grandchildren will heap on us as the final curtain comes down.

Meanwhile, we will eat and defecate and copulate and cavil as if there was no tomorrow ... and take cruises and vote for idiots and throw garbage in the oceans and burn fossil fuels and drive giant SUVs and ....

The status quo is a perpetual-motion nightmare from which we must rouse, or it will extinguish our dreams. We keep looking for ourselves in the cosmos's endless void and finding nothing but billions of sepulchers in which our fancies are entombed. There is no one else out there. Humankind is a unique and unrepeatable biological phenomenon forever destined to ponder the enigma of its absurd existence. The mission of sane men is not to reach for the stars but to embrace their home planet and strive toward civility and peace. Fat chance.

♦

Time out. People say, perhaps hastily, perhaps metaphorically, that *"the years go by."* They don't and certainly not of their own volition. Time is directionally neutral. It is not in motion. It is we who traverse it. We let the years slip through our fingers while pretending to be living. The human brain is unaware of the tricks it plays on itself.

TWO MILLENNIA AND COUNTING — About 65 percent of humans believe in a *"god,"* spirit, supernatural entity. The pantheon of deities is crowded. The most popular is invisible, deaf, mute (but omniscient and almighty), an essence inhabiting the nether regions of the cosmos whose fury and vindictiveness is unequaled (but he loves us …). Others are carved out of wood, sculpted out of granite, or molded from clay, others yet are unseen but said to be perched on the highest mountains, inhabiting the deepest lakes, haunting the most impenetrable forests. Some cultures worshipped cats, ibises and baboons, crocodiles and fish, mongooses, shrews, dogs, and jackals, serpents, beetles, eels, and bulls. In Hinduism the monkey deity, Hanuman, is a prominent figure. He is a reincarnation of Shiva, the god of destruction. Go figure.

Many people also believe that once they trash this planet and die, they will be teleported to a *"better place"* which they will likely proceed to devastate. Religion has been fostering apocalypse as a logical end of its world model and earthly existence, and generations have been raised to invoke it, not prevent it. Would *"God"* be willing to create another world for us if we fail to save this one? He'd be a fool if he did.

If we can blame one institution for our demise (other than banks, corporations, gun merchants, and governments), it's religion. Religion teaches that there is a better world out there, an Eden full of angels, pick-up trucks, moonshine, guns, and free fat-dripping triple cheeseburgers. Religion openly teaches us not to give a shit about Earth *("Thou art strangers in this world.")*. If life is just a stopover on the way to our permanent celestial abode, why bother to protect the world we live in? For two thousand years we have been waiting for the Second Landing. It did not happen. The navigator got drunk, plotted the wrong course, and slammed the vessel into the razor-sharp extrusions of a shallow reef.

Religion insists that a talking ape has transcendental value in the Universe. While a talking ape is in fact an interesting phenomenon—though not as innocent or deserving of mercy as the great apes that came before him—his worth has been seriously overestimated. The Universe will do fine without us.

PARTY ANIMALS?—I was thinking. I'm not a model of civic virtue. I'll wage war against injustice, lies, and corruption but I'm not a joiner, have no need or desire to *"belong"* and find it hard to understand why people whose only link is a common residential tract, a city, or a nation effusively seek each other's company. I must be a freak. Thankfully, I live with a woman who shares my aversion of crowds, noise, and small talk.

Sociologists insist that humans are gregarious party animals, and that society is built on interconnections between groups and individuals motivated by common interests, objectives ... and even phobias. What makes me such a pariah? Mind you, I'm not complaining. I consider this anomaly quite ... ordinary. It's the herd instinct that I find aberrant. It's an impulse I have never felt. I don't bother asking myself why. Does an ant ask itself why it's not a butterfly?

HOMO HOMINIS LUPUS — Unfortunately, *"interfaith dialogue,"* like world diplomacy, works only when rational people are willing to sit down and iron out their differences. Terrorists, religious fanatics, and deranged individuals are like rocks. Have you ever tried to reason with a rock? Nothing you say can change their uncompromising stance. What we need is a global revolution of conscience whereby societies consciously engage in the dismantling of the political, economic, social structures that stifle democracy. So long as democracy allows the existence and proliferation of undemocratic ideas and institutions that plot its demise, such a moral/intellectual rebellion is improbable unless a militant democracy acts decisively against those who would threaten it. *Homo hominis lupus* (man is a wolf to man).*

♦

I can imagine tourists from another galaxy visiting a dried-up, dead Earth, finding the remnants of human civilizations, and commenting, *"These bipedal creatures must have had a great sense of humor. In five hundred years they transitioned from throwing children and virgins into volcanoes to committing ecocide and killing each other. Hilarious."*

---

* With deepest apologies to wolves.

ANTI-COMMUNIST HYSTERIA — A myth cultivated by French revisionists proclaims that Algeria was French. No. Algeria was a miserable colony whose citizens — about ten million — were held in a humiliating stranglehold of political, economic, social, and cultural inferiority by an elite of less than a million French settlers for more than a century.

France built schools and hospitals, but most Algerians did not enjoy the rights or privileges granted their master colonizers. The degradation felt by the colonized stemmed less from the iniquity of their circumstances than from the symbolic and real rank of inferiority imposed by the usurper. The splitting of colonial society into two divergent domains — the conqueror and the conquered — lasted until the 1960s. It is true that Algerian Jews were granted French citizenship, but it was denied to Muslims who were also banned from the ballot boxes. When rigged elections triggered demonstrations, censorship, arrests, extrajudicial executions, and kidnappings followed.

In November 1954 (I was in Paris at the time studying journalism) seventy simultaneous terrorist attacks against the *"Pieds Noirs"* [*Black Feet*, the French born in Algeria during the period of French rule] led to an ugly and bloody war of independence. Shortly before, France, soon to be replaced by an Amerika plagued by anti-communist hysteria, had abandoned Indochina following a bitter and futile war that culminated in a scathing defeat at Dien Bien Phu. The French debacle in its colonies of Vietnam, Laos, and Cambodia, and its loss of prestige internationally, inspired nationalist fervor among the French, especially those born in Algeria who considered it their own. France dispatched a large contingent of Foreign Legionnaires; army conscripts followed. Accounts of misbehavior by French soldiers circulated freely in the capital, as were the disturbing revelations that many French had been massacred. It was also learned that Algerian women had been raped, that men were beaten, immersed in icy water, showered with excrement, and electrocuted (a treatment that my late father, a resistance fighter, endured at the hands of the French Gestapo during his arrest at Fresnes Prison). Declassified documents, including photos and a glut of press reports, books, and documentaries shed a heartbreaking light on the atrocities committed by the French in Algeria.

Maurice Papon (decorated by De Gaulle in 1961) will be remembered as the secretary general of the Bordeaux police during the Second World War. He participated in the deportation of more than 1,600 Jews. He is also known for his activities in the Algerian War, during which he tortured insurgent Algerian prisoners and ordered the severe repression of a pro-National Liberation Front demonstration against a curfew he had imposed.

Refusing to admit defeat, the Algerians fought valiantly and lost more than five hundred thousand fighters during the eight-year conflict. The hostilities ended with the independence of Algeria and the annihilation of the French colonial empire. Many in France still mourn the loss of Algeria which, predictably, they blame on *"communism."*

As long as lions don't have their own historians, the history of hunting will always glorify the hunter.

REQUIEM FOR A FUTURE PAST — Rebellion is the logical response to real or perceived threats; words must be followed with action. So far, only the young are speaking out, marching, demanding concrete change. A youth movement that started with a teenager in Sweden spread across the globe recently, evidenced by the students from London to New Delhi who skipped school to take part in demonstrations calling for action on climate change.

The adults are sitting on their hands and, other than the scientists whose warnings no one heeds, the only segment of society aware of the Earth's impending demise are those most likely to face it. In that sense, the future of mankind (if any) is in the hands of the world's youth. Whether their collective voice is being heard loudly enough and whether their appeals and supplications will lead to any concrete change is another story. But at least, they're trying. Their elders are either saying and doing nothing or denouncing the young activists as deluded troublemakers.

♦

I dreamed I heard a song the other night. I didn't understand the lyrics, they were otherworldly, but the tune was exquisite and haunting, a mixture of melancholy and hope, of quiet optimism and serene resignation. Only angels could have composed the melody, I thought. I found it fitting that a chorus of bright, young women sang it with enchanting sweetness. It sounded like a psalm, a lullaby, and a requiem. It reminded me of the songs of hope that women sang in Hitler's extermination camps before they were starved to death or gassed — a canticle and a farewell to life. It's the kind of song that might have been taken aboard the Voyager 1 spacecraft in 1977, along with Bach, Beethoven, and Mozart, as mankind's ultimate expression of melancholy and sorrow for a near-comatose Earth. The melody lingered in my mind's ear long after I awoke.

NO REVOLUTION WITHOUT A *REVOLUTION*—I read an *Extinction Rebellion* article the other day. I fully endorse its recommendations—many of which parallel those put forward in the *Green New Deal*, the economic stimulus bill sponsored by Rep. Alexandria Ocasio-Cortez (D-NY) and Sen. Ed Markey (D-MA) which addresses climate change and economic inequality. My gut feeling is that the Extinction Rebellion movement has as much a chance of succeeding as the Green New Deal, not because its proposals are meritless or unworkable, on the contrary, but because there is little will to implement such radical changes, even if three percent of the electorate (circa nine million) join the fight. Republicans claim there is no money to finance such sweeping changes. Of course, that's a lie. The US is flush with money but it's in the wrong pockets and no unstoppable force can nudge such immovable object as the instinct to protect corporate wealth. Capitalism is the predominant religion, and any hint of reform is viewed as Socialist heresy and either ignored or violently rejected.

I also believe that the future of Amerika is in the hands of women. Alas this Davidic fifth column is no match for the heartless Goliaths it pits itself against. There will be a lot of noise. Some minor token concessions might even be accorded to placate the radical elements of the movement but any concrete measure to reduce pollution worldwide will fail, especially since the efforts in one area of the globe are nullified by super polluters in another.

There can be no revolution without a *revolution*. Given the brevity of life, mankind's narcissism, greed, indifference, instinct of preservation, and gross social and economic inequality, the kind of revolution needed to transform humanity from a taker into a giver is the stuff of romantic fiction. As historian Jacques

Barzun writes, *"There is no 'legitimacy' in revolution; power belongs to whoever can seize it."**

♦

The conquistadors committed horrific crimes. But to blame Columbus, as millions of Latin Americans do every year on his anniversary, and as Jacques Barzun suggests, *"is an exercise in retrospective lynching."* Columbus, the product of his time, may not have been the heartless ghoul his detractors claim. It would be unfair to suggest that the victims of the Conquista were peaceable or harmless. By the time Columbus reached the "New World," the mighty Aztec, Mayan, and Inca empires were already crumbling, victims of domestic wars, a culture of death, bloody inter-tribal feuds, corruption, colossal mismanagement of dwindling natural resources, and crippling climate change. Their descendants, several million strong but socially marginalized and politically inert, rail at Columbus as the single agent of their five-century-long misfortunes because railing against their modern oppressors — all as dishonest, inept, and apathetic as their feather-adorned and drug-addicted ancient "governors" — would cost them their freedom, if not their lives.

I have watched them, year after year on October 14, trekking from their fog-shrouded hilltop hamlets to the cities, marching silently and symbolically against the Genoese sailor, but actually protesting, a sullen expression on their copper faces, against the modern governments that oppress them, marginalize them.

"We don't really give a shit about Columbus," a young Mayan tribal counselor told me in private,

"We're protesting five hundred years of cultural alienation, depersonalization, and persecution that we continue to endure, in his name, by his political successors. The last time we questioned

---

* From Dawn to Decadence — 500 Years of Western Cultural Life.

the legitimacy of the government, we were met by truncheon-wielding Cobra Commandos."

And I watched them slogging back to their hamlets bloodied and dispirited.

A revolution is long overdue but it won't take place so long as the US maintains its political and economic stranglehold on nations that cannot afford to disobey the big bully Mafia state to the north and so long as the ten-or-so all-powerful oligarchic families that own and run everything kiss the bully's ass in return for keeping their ill-gotten gains and preserving the Babylonian lifestyle to which they're accustomed. It takes a *Revolution* to achieve a revolution. People who are forced to choose between tyranny and death often opt for the former.

◆

Skipping *"history class"* is a healthy way of putting parts of the past away. After all, the past is gone. It cannot be resuscitated, revised, or mended. It belongs in that mental file cabinet where we store the bric-a-brac and curios of a bygone era. Living in the present with an eye peeled toward the future is far more practical than lusting for or lamenting the past. Still, it is useful to remember that the past tends to leach into the present, and that yesterday might have had a direct and cumulative influence on the dynamics that shape our current reality. The key is to be able to access memories, as one does a photo album, without being overcome or saddled by the images they send back.

Life is filled with cause-and-effect events. I have suffered from intermittent bouts of melancholy since I was a child. Much of it was the inevitable aftermath of the things I witnessed and endured during and after the Second World War. The rest was brought on by hasty decisions and blunders I bitterly regretted. I have since learned to pretend not to worry about the things over which I have no control. My melancholy is existential, not clinical (I am displeased with various aspects of my life) but I manage to keep things in check by sheer force of will. I'm not interested in spending years on the couch exploring my life in the womb. Fortunately, I have an imaginative nature that finds in painting and writing a means of releasing and exploiting creative emotions. I am in distinguished company: Woody Allen, Edgar Degas, Dostoyevsky, Goya, Stephen King, Michelangelo, Isaac Newton, and Leo Tolstoy, to name a few, also battled depression. They might not have been the intellectual prodigies for which they are hailed without it. Not that I consider myself a prodigy.

AN ASSUMPTION IS NOT A FACT—I often hear, *"I am entitled to my opinion"*--an incongruity with which any opposition to an absurd idea is put down by pretending that one has the right to disfigure the truth. It is uttered either out of ignorance or stupidity, or, more wickedly, to defend factually indefensible positions. An opinion is defined as a view or judgment formed about something. Not necessarily based on fact or knowledge, it's a personal belief, an attitude that rests on grounds insufficient to produce complete certainty. In other words, it's a conjecture, a hypothesis, an assumption.

Newton's law of gravity wasn't based on an opinion; it was a deduction grounded on observation and repeatable experiments. When Einstein formulated his relativity theories, he wasn't hypothesizing; his was a mental construct based on the totality of certain scientific facts he knew to be true. $E=mc2$ is not an opinion; it's an empirical reality.

Opinions are rarely original. We adopt them, we cling to them because independent and critical thought requires an enormous capital of intellectual latitude and moral courage, not to mention a gray matter uncontaminated by immovable beliefs. Instead, we shamelessly peddle them while being convinced of our own deductive faculties. The great tragedy is that few of us care about the lies that opinions might conceal. They are the dungeons in which we lock ourselves by feigning a clear conscience—very often the result of a bad memory. Most of our beliefs are built on a vast scaffolding of dogmas, doctrines, prejudices, and chimeras often advanced by someone else. And yet we believe that they are the result of our own ruminations because they protect us from what we fear most—reality.

Everybody has opinions. Naïve, harmless, or wacky, they are easily dismissed. Inflexible or toxic, they blind us, inflate us with arrogance. Taken to the extreme, they drive us insane. Opining from emotion does the truth a disservice. It just makes us feel better about ourselves because, heavens forbid, we should be wrong about anything that comes out unreflexively from our mouths. Opinions are not worth the breath on whose gossamer wings they are carried. And yet, they're the devices with which the truth is often sacrificed. Without them there would be nothing to talk about.

AN UNLIKELY CANDIDATE— Any suggestion that my discourses betray repressed political ambitions confuses their fervor with an urge to join this, the ugliest cabal of greedy profiteers — politicians — egomaniacs whose sole objectives are power, not truth, influence, not justice, self-enrichment, not egalitarianism, and whose only raison-d'être is to put themselves in a position to do major thieving. I can affirm without fear of contradiction that my spartan upbringing, utter lack of self-importance, lifelong disdain for money, congenital inability to earn it and, once earned, to hold on to it or make it grow, are not the attributes of a successful thief ... or politician.

◆

On the eve of Joe Biden's inauguration, it would be useful to pause and recollect that Donald J. Trump is a consummate crook. The key question voters needed to ponder as they were headed to the polls or mailed in their paper ballots was whether his assorted crimes — phenomenal and largely unchallenged prevarications, obstructionist directives, conspiracy to violate campaign finance statutes with payoffs to two women of dubious morals, his grifter's use of the White House for personal profit, his bank account in China, a country he keeps vilifying, his politics of anger, division, and vengeance — rose to the high crimes and misdemeanors definition required by the extreme constitutional remedy of impeachment ... which he deservedly earned but which had no effect on his fans. Voters also needed to plumb their conscience and concede, after four years of chaotic, not to say deranged governance, that his lawless administration had to be perforce terminated Many fiercely rejected the idea. Many more, coming to their senses, helped turn the tide.

◆

Implying that my perorations conceal some impulse to run for office is as comical as it is baseless. The radical changes I would push for make me patently unelectable in Amerika ... not to mention a prime target for assassination. Here is where I stand on some issues. Perhaps President Biden agrees.

The economy — the wealth and resources of a country — may be good for the affluent, but it's not so great for the average working stiff. If the economy is so *"solid,"* as Trump would have us believe, why were my Social Security benefits *"adjusted"* by only $12 in 2020 while the cost of living keeps soaring, while Amazon's Jeff Bezos adds $13 billion in one day to his net worth and pays no taxes, and while 30 million workers depend on unemployment checks that are held hostage by rich politicians? Why is there plenty of money to keep US troops in 80 countries around the world, or subsidize the next Moon mission? Why do CEOs earn astronomical year-end bonuses, but most families cannot survive on one salary — that is if they still have a job?

An "economy" is good only when the lowest echelons of society can afford the necessities of life. My first initiative would be to impose price controls on all basic commodities essential to the daily sustenance and well-being of the citizenry. That would include food, healthcare, medicines, education, and public transportation. The cost of a loaf of bread, a stick of butter, a dozen eggs, a gallon of milk, a head of lettuce would be the same nationwide. I would tax luxury items that only the rich can afford at 500 percent. I would raise the minimum wage to reflect the artificially inflated and fraudulent cost of living so that a family of four can live in reasonable comfort and dignity on the salary of a single wage-earner, as was the case when I first arrived in Amerika in 1956. Lunch counters, restrooms, and water fountains were still segregated but if you were white, literate, and gainfully employed, life was a bowl of cherries. If you lost your job you could find a better-paying one the next day. To quote Samuel Johnson (1709-1784), the country has since become *"a place of great wealth and dreadful wickedness, a den of tyrants, and a dungeon of [economically underprivileged] slaves."*

"Representative democracy" is a form of political redlining; the Electoral College is an anachronism, a flawed system, and a disgrace. Both violate the core tenet of democracy that all votes count equally. What's the point of holding an election if a convoluted and devious calculus allows the candidate finishing second to be declared the winner? Both must be abolished and replaced with universal suffrage—one man, one vote. Gerrymandering, a diabolical scheme designed to shift the balance of power along racial or economic lines, should also be outlawed. The two-party system—both parties at best apathetic to meaningful change and, at worst, downright hostile to reform—should be augmented and enriched with parties that, while striving for national unity and coherence, reflect the distinct ideologies of a multiracial, multicultural society. To encourage full participation, elections should take place on weekends.

The Second Amendment, a misguided and hastily scripted addendum ratified in 1791 in favor of maintaining *"a well-regulated Militia,"* but in no way legalizing individual arms-bearing rights, should be revised. Gun ownership shall be granted to adults with clean records and certified to be in full possession of their faculties. The sale—and purchase—of assault weapons must be prohibited.

As novelist and New York University professor Jonathan Safran Foer aptly remarks, *"hunting for sport is just about as vile as humans can get."* It shall be banned except in areas of the country where it is the only means of survival.

Absolute separation between State and Church shall be enforced. Religious institutions shall be stripped of their tax-exempt status and mandated to pay taxes like everyone else. Houses of worship will survive on the charity of the parishioners; they shall own no businesses nor engage in commercial endeavors. Any attempt by faith-based entities to muscle in on the body politic and influence court decisions, to sway elections, manipulate education or dictate a faith-based code of conduct shall be forcefully resisted and penalized. The phrase, *"under God,"* lobbied for by ultra-Catholics and added to the Pledge of Allegiance in 1954, shall be deleted. Freedom of religion is meaningless unless it includes freedom *from* religion.

The Supreme Court, the steadfast patron of the rich and powerful, the unelected enemy of democracy, shall be tasked with adjudicating on the basis or law, not partisan politics, or the justices' ideological leanings. As *The Nation* editor, D. D. Guttenplan writes in a recent editorial,

> *"Unlike the blindfolded figure of Justice, the Supreme Court has a long history of blindness only on one side: the left."*

Justices shall be voted in, not appointed. They shall serve for a period not exceeding seven years, with a mandatory retirement age of 65.

Wars shall neither be declared nor prosecuted without the full assent of the voters through plebiscites or national referenda.

States' "rights" are shyster politics that regularly deny their citizens equal treatment under the law. They are at their ruthless worst in the most regressive and backward Southern, Great Plains, and Mountain states. The notion that states should enjoy special privileges by enacting their own laws is absurd. Says Dr. Ronald Feinman, professor of American History, Government and Politics:

> *"Conservatives and Republicans love to promote states' rights, and for good reason. It allows states to deny their citizens the same rights, privileges, and benefits other states provide. Historically, it allowed states to have slaves; to promote segregation; to sanction capital punishment; to show no concern for the poor; to exploit labor through 'right to work' laws; to destroy the environment for industrial benefit; to victimize women and children; and to deny*

basic health care expansion under Medicaid and the Affordable Care Act."

"Eminent domain," the right of government to expropriate private land for public use, is a system that is easily abused. It creates the foundation for mass evictions; *"fair compensation"* is rarely fair. When not deemed in the interest of national security, this self-granted government practice shall be subject to stringent exclusion clauses. For example, a farm shall not be expropriated, nor a nature preserve commandeered to create a golf course, a resort, or mass-occupancy tenements.

Amerika's educational system needs to be revamped. Multiple-choice tests in history, geography, civics, and languages will be replaced with written essays and oral exams. And penmanship will count! Math problems will be solved manually (no calculators allowed) by demonstrating sequentially from premise to final answer how that answer was reached. History books shall be purged from the lies or omissions that instill a false or misleading image of Amerika's racist, imperialist, warmongering past. Teacher salaries shall be raised to give one of the most underrated professions the reverence it deserves. Public schools shall be enjoined from conducting prayers, a devotional exercise that belongs in the home or house of worship, not in the classroom.

Print and electronic mass communication media carrying product or political advertisements known to contain lies or produced to misinform or confuse the public shall be subject to heavy fines.

Artistic, cultural, and educational institutions (theaters, museums, concert halls, opera houses, seats of higher learning) will benefit from generous government subsidies as they are essential in redressing Amerika's climate of anti-intellectualism and a pervasive disdain of scholarship.

People wishing to get married will have their heads examined, as will those planning to bring children into this world. Candidates for matrimony and parenthood will have to prove that they are compatible as well as financially and emotionally fit to raise children who do not ask to be born. Alimony shall be granted based on proven necessity, not codified tradition.

To reverse extreme concentrations of wealth and help usher a new era of participatory democratic socialism, federal taxes shall be raised to subsidize a national health system that protects every citizen, from the cradle to the grave, without the intervention of predatory insurance companies. To restrain the largest fortunes from getting any larger, all income, including capital gains, dividends, and rents will be assessed at 90 percent. It's unjust when those who *own* have all the power and those who *labor* have none. Workers shall have a say in how enterprises are run. The National Labor Relations Board shall be revamped to arbitrate legitimate disputes between management and labor—not to undermine workers. Proceeds from wealth and inheritance taxes will be used to give a universal capital endowment of $150,000 to every citizen who turns 25.

No paper-pusher in Washington will ever tell physicians how to practice medicine.

Last, I would encourage the adoption of a constitutional amendment which would defend the rights of atheists and declare atheistic worldview as deserving protection from hordes of religious freaks. The Constitution (grudgingly) protects gays. Why not atheists?

Perhaps Joe Biden can oblige so I don't have to run for office.

ONE NATION UNDER STRESS—Last night I watched a disturbing documentary produced by Dr. Sanjay Gupta, the noted neurosurgeon and CNN chief medical correspondent. Titled, *One Nation Under Stress*, the program focused on the number of deaths in the US from cirrhosis of the liver, opioid addiction overdoses, and suicide—all blamed on the increasing existential pressures to which we are subjected. Suicides went up 30% in the last twenty years.

At the same time, life expectancy in the US dropped for the third year in a row due to a unique blend of fears and anxieties that trigger depression, despair, anger, alcoholism, drug addiction, and violence. Add the proliferation of firearms to the mix and the situation gets out of hand. The Washington, DC-based Gun Violence Archive think tank reported more than 2,000 deaths by shooting in Amerika between March 1 and April 19, 2020—a 16 percent increase over the average in the same period during the past three years. This is what occurred during the 1918-19 flu pandemic, when murders soared. Sheltering in place can put people in a foul mood.

◆

Sadly, I never felt quite at ease in the US, perhaps because I was 19 when my parents shipped me here, because I was not fleeing Europe or seeking to make a fortune, perhaps because life in Amerika, for those not accustomed to its rituals, values, idiosyncrasies, and frenetic pace—or unwilling to endure them—can be erosive. Luckily, I do not have an addictive personality. In fact, I have a congenital intolerance to alcohol and an aversion to pill-popping. I was in the Navy when I got drunk for the first and last time. I was sick as a dog. Never again. I experimented briefly with marijuana, but quickly tired of its cataleptic effects. My melancholia, if I can call it that, stems from an inability, after 65 years in this country, to cross an immense ideological and cultural chasm, not to mention the fierce climate of competitiveness, and the ravaging emphasis on *"performance."*

◆

In Amerika, you're only as good as your last success or *"what have you done for me lately...?"* As the visionary director, Erich von Stroheim once remarked,

> *"If you live in France, for instance, and you have written one good book, or painted one good picture, or directed one outstanding film fifty years ago and nothing else since, you are still recognized and honored. People take their hats off to you and call you 'maître'. They do not forget. In Hollywood you're only as good as your last picture. If you didn't have one in production within the last three months, you're forgotten, no matter what you have achieved before."*

It is not untimely to suggest that stress has a psychologically destructive effect on an already compromised psyche, nor is it premature to predict that a form of self-destructive psychosis — not the nonconformity of geniuses and virtuosos but the lunacy of greedy, violent, *"performers,"* combined with the willful ignorance and apathy of idiots — could contribute to Amerika's demise.

There is a point at which normalcy is a sign of mental decay. That's when the brain turns to shit. Shit is a useful fertilizer but what germinates from this foul excretion is not brains.

THE BELLY OF THE BEAST—I can still hear the rancor, taste the venom when President Trump, proving yet again that he is a bigot and a nativist, bounced off an adoring crowd of salivating chauvinists a warning to immigrants and asylum seekers, *"There's no room. The country's full. Go home."*

You will recall the details of our transcontinental odyssey. Anyone who has driven cross-country will agree that Amerika is magnificent. One striking and haunting memory of this coast-to-coast expedition is the vast stretches of barren geography—thousands of square miles of nothingness, from horizon to horizon, from sunup to sundown, deserted if spectacular expanses of utter emptiness as far as the eye can see. Gee, I mused as we rolled along Interstate 10 … there's a lot of vacant space. There's a lot of room in these uninhabited stretches of fallow geography.

◆

I spent twelve years (from 1994 to 2006) on assignment in Central America where I covered politics, the military, human rights, and other socio-economic issues. I may use metaphor and allegory in my works of fiction because it's one way of telling inconvenient truths through the medium of literature. In opposition, my journalism has always been literal and blunt. I try not to speculate. I don't fabricate facts. I don't indulge in opinion except in columns clearly labelled as such—and even then, they are anchored in verifiable fact, not rumor or innuendo.

Battered by decades of civil strife and all-out war, Central America—notably El Salvador, Guatemala, Honduras, and Nicaragua--remains a region rocked by political chaos, plagued by economic decay, and convulsed by horrific violence and state-sponsored human rights abuses. Lurking in the shadows, former military strongmen itching for a comeback and feeble, hopelessly inept and corrupt civilian puppet regimes continue to frustrate efforts to bring some semblance of democracy and justice through much needed reforms.

Gross inequality in wealth and status—a dozen or so dynastic families rule Guatemala and Honduras, the countries I know most intimately. They own the banks, the media, utilities, communications, and transportation networks. They are the most violent and dissolute nations in this hemisphere, the only countries where my investigative reports earned me death threats. Children are routinely being abandoned or expelled by families that obey the Church's mandate to *"multiply and populate the earth."* Regrettably, while the Church voices sanctimonious concern for the unborn, it does nothing on behalf of those who are out of the womb. At any given time, there are an estimated 75,000 minors roaming the streets of Central America—orphans, runaways from households eroded by overcrowding, poverty, alcoholism, and drug addiction, children abandoned or cast out by parents no longer able to provide. The streets are their permanent habitat. Viewed as *"vermin," "a blight," "parasites,"* and *"criminals,"* by the state, they are considered *"bad for tourism, bad for the neighborhood," "bad for the nation's image."* Trumpeted by indifferent and openly hostile regimes, these sinister portrayals have inspired a wave of bloodletting against these children that persists to this day. Once reactive and sporadic, intimidation, threats, illegal arrest and detention, vicious beatings, torture, rape, and extra-judicial executions at the hand of law-enforcement agents and private security have now become routine. An apathetic legal system, lazy attorneys, and bribable judges all turn a blind eye and almost never convict these criminals.

There is another dimension to the lingering despair plaguing Central America—the enduring legacy and impact of a little known, secretive, and infamous military institution, The US

Army School of the Americas (SOA), long since rechristened the Western Hemisphere Institute for Security Cooperation, a name change that did nothing to alter, let alone expiate, its ghoulish past. Founded in 1946 in Panama, sponsored and trained by the CIA, it has sired some of the region's most bloodthirsty tyrants and is singly responsible for years of persecution, ethnocide, and US-inspired political and economic destabilization. Now billeted at Fort Benning in Columbus, Georgia, the school has trained more than 60,000 Latin American and Caribbean Basin officers and enlisted men. It has also spawned hundreds of thugs, many of whom were charged with the wholesale torture, murder, rape, and *"disappearance"* of farmers, liberal clergy, trade unionists, teachers, students, human rights advocates, and journalists — charged but never brought to trial. Others were implicated in narcotrafficking and money-laundering schemes. Typically, the US overlooked their crimes when the perceived hemispheric enemy was *"communism."* Many, to help them evade prosecution by the International Court, have since been granted asylum in the US, and are now basking like sated iguanas in the Florida, Louisiana, and Texas sun. The most notorious alumni include:

- Omar Torrijos of Panama, Guillermo Rodriguez of Ecuador and Juan Velasco Alvarado of Peru — all implicated in the violent overthrew of constitutionally elected civilian governments.

- Leopoldo Galtieri, ex-head of Argentina's junta — defeated in the Falklands "Dirty War" against the British. A CIA asset, Galtieri helped establish Honduras' death squad, Battalion 3-16.

- Hugo Banzer Suarez, Bolivian president in the 1970s — crushed dissident clerics and suppressed militant tin miners with savage zeal.

- Roberto D'Aubuisson, the late Salvadoran death-squad leader — plotted the assassination of Archbishop Romero and engineered the El Mozote massacre of 900 men, women, and children.

- Manuel Noriega, ex-dictator of Panama and a CIA asset pampered by the US until his handlers no longer considered him useful..

- Honduran generals Humberto Regalado Hernandez (linked to Colombian drug cartels) and Policarpo Paz Garcia (led a corrupt regime in the 80s).

- Manuel Antonio Callejas y Callejas — chief of Guatemalan intelligence in the late 1970s and early 1980s, when thousands of political opponents were assassinated.

- Gen. Jose Efrain Rios Montt. A former president of Guatemala (1982-83) Montt is best remembered for his *"beans or bullets"* policy — beans for the obedient, bullets for the rest.

One of the principal lessons the tragic history of Central America can teach is that the blood of the innocent, the vulnerable, the dispossessed, can be shed with impunity. Twelve years in the belly of the beast, twelve years of engaged journalism during which I did my best to inform, stir, and inspire, all for naught. My work produced little more than fleeting acknowledgements by a precious few, a storm of resentment, angry ad-hominem attacks by many, and the monumental indifference of the rest. The multitudes desperate to leave El Salvador, Guatemala, and Honduras, *"the tired, the poor, the huddled masses yearning to breathe free"* are tragic reminders that things have not only not changed but they are worse than ever.

In a blistering indictment of the prevailing climate of racism and xenophobia that fuel hatred and violence, distinguished historian, Paul Johnson, reminds us that *"people matter more than concepts and must come first. The worst despotism,"* he warns, *"is the heartless tyranny of ideas"* — a theme reprised by Timothy Snyder in his latest manifesto.[*]

◆

I was baffled by the absence of any reference to the US Army School of the Americas in a recent article in *The Nation*, entitled, "Washington Trained Guatemala's Killers."

The author's failure to credit the SOA for all the horrific crimes perpetrated in Guatemala and elsewhere in the Isthmus by America's lackeys is disheartening, even more so since *The Nation*'s editors did not bother to challenge the author or engage in exhaustive fact-checking.

---

[*] On Tyranny © 2017, Crown Publishing.

A TROUBLING DEFICIT—The problem with education in Amerika is that it is highly regulated at the state level. What Arkansas teaches about the Civil War (if anything remotely resembling the truth...) is quite different from what Massachusetts history books might reveal. Even public libraries are monitored by the state, sometimes even by individual counties. Books available at the New York Public Library might be banned in Georgia or Kansas. One of my books was banned by the Kern County (California) public library ... without explanation. I suspect the county's morality police must have objected to any of several anti-clerical jabs, perhaps this one:

> *"I've known religious people of every faith. Underneath the ecstasy, the jubilation, and the hallelujahs lurk dark fears and self-doubts and unanswered prayers that the faithful sheepishly attribute to God's 'strange and mysterious ways.' Most corrosive is the subconscious fear of lapsing convictions, an-ever present state of mind that sends the faithful to extremes of religiosity — ritualistic, mechanical, frenzied. Such people are to be pitied because that's all they have in life. What appears to be euphoria is in fact repressed anxiety. I have also known people who never went to church but quietly, anonymously worshiped God (or some undefinable 'Grand Architect of the Universe') in the temple of their own mind. For some, religion without histrionics is meaningless. The Mass is the perfect example of a flamboyant theatrical production. It's free entertainment."*

Amerika may be the richest, most powerful nation on earth, but it is one of the most intellectually repressed. The coastal outer ring of urbane, progressive cities (Boston, New York, Philadelphia, Miami, Houston, Los Angeles, San Francisco, Portland, and Seattle) does not represent the heartland, which has remained hopelessly blinkered, stubbornly conservative, and fanatically religious.

I'm not surprised that kids in the US know close to nothing about the Holocaust. Most know even less about the methodical slaughter of Native Americans, slavery, the Civil War, the calculated annulment of rights painfully earned during Reconstruction, Jim Crow, segregation, and other shocking expressions of Amerika's centuries' old disregard for justice and equality. Ironically, many teachers are just as ignorant on a whole spectrum of topics. I remember my teachers: Highly educated, they were licensed to teach everything from Algebra to Zoology. It's not the case here. I know some teachers. I shall not impugn their devotion or skill but their illiteracy in certain subjects is staggering. The blame must also be shared with a new generation of students whose only passions are smartphones, selfies, social media, video games, and early unprotected sex.

THERMOSTAT GONE WILD — The coronavirus may cause a fever, but at the same time it is bringing down a fever that has lasted for 300 years. The industrial revolution brought this planet to an unhealthy, feverish state: overpopulation, pollution, global warming, ecological degradation, habitat destruction, and resource exhaustion. Reacting like an infected organism that has lost its internal balance, the planet's thermostat responded: The climate began to change.

But this was only the symptom. The planet is much more intelligent. Like humans, it has an immune system that consists of all the meteorological, biotic, and abiotic processes that constantly cycle, collect information, and monitor its health. These processes are perpetually interconnected. They balance each other in such a way that, if one thing goes wrong, if something seems to be out of kilter, such as increases in carbon dioxide or temperature, other processes are triggered down the chain of command until a solution is found to bring the system back into balance. The process may be complicated, and it may take a while in human years to respond, but don't be fooled: Nature has eyes everywhere on the planet and responds in mysterious and unpredictable ways.

While there is to date no evidence that Covid-19 is a direct consequence of climate change, those who fail to consider that possibility do not understand the complexity and interdependence of Earth's ecosystems. It is a complexity that baffles even the most expert Earth scientists whose findings and predictions about climate change are nothing short of alarming. The planet's immune system is super-intelligent. It may have taken a while, but it managed to finally pinpoint the sole culprit: a species known as Homo sapiens. Earth has found us, and it is trying to chasten us with the most precise therapy it could find, a molecule that is specific to our DNA, not unlike how gene therapy works. It is a virus that hunts humans and kills primarily humans.

It's time we begin to recognize how intuitive our planet really is. For us it may seem that 300 years is a delayed response. But in geologic temporal scales, Earth figured us out in no time. Yet we continue to disrespect it, to treat it as non-sentient, simply because it doesn't have a Twitter account. Well, it has finally sent us a message: For the time being, stay away from other humans.

ON TYRANNY—Timothy Snyder's book is elegantly written and filled with timeless wisdom, truths, and persuasive warnings. I did take exception at the author's casual use of the word *"communism,"* a word that I always write or utter circumscribed by quotation marks. Sadly, given man's cupidity and egotism, the Marxist ideals that could have turned mankind into a family rather than ceaselessly warring factions have never left the printed page. What has passed for *"communism"* in Russia and Eastern Europe, China, Cuba, Venezuela, Nicaragua, and elsewhere is nothing but a heavy-handed, ruthless, tyrannical system of governance in which the individual is sacrificed at the altar of the party. The only communities where a semblance of the *"communist"* model has ever been successfully applied are Israeli cooperatives known as kibbutzim and monasteries. I wish the author had made that distinction in his otherwise superb commentary on the ideological threats that face society.

In Senator Joseph McCarthy's America in the 1950s, artistic non-conformism, secularism, and a penchant for social justice were also seen as unmistakable signs of *"communist"* tendencies by far-right demagogues. Popular liberation movements aimed at shaking the yoke of colonialism were slandered, as were those who opposed US military *"interventions"* in Vietnam, Yugoslavia, Iraq, Afghanistan, Panama, and Grenada. John Lennon's pro-peace Platonic activism was also attributed to *"communist tendencies"* that his accusers knew to be false. Had they lived today, Thomas Paine and the poet Henry David Thoreau would also be declared *"communists."* The aggressive investment strategies and bold manipulations that characterize capitalism are called *"progressive"* although they weaken the middle class and harm the poor. The Nazis and *"communists"* persecuted the Freemasons; some called them "Bolsheviks" others accused the ancient fraternity of being an agent of Western imperialism. Everything is semantic. But it takes scoundrels to corrupt it and idiots to believe it without defining the variants and innuendos.

There is another problem. What passes for *"communism"* has perverted the paradigm it purports to symbolize and betrayed the objectives outlined in *Das Kapital*. Instead of addressing urgent social problems — inequality, poverty, injustice, hunger, and illiteracy — the *"communist"* crusade resorted to an apostolate of terror that belied its Utopian fantasies while claiming millions of lives. In the end, the rules of the game of *"communism,"* as are the commands of religion, are unenforceable because they are incompatible with human nature. There is much to regret about the abject failure of *"communism's"* noblest ideals. As the late historian, Charles Van Doren, suggests,

> *"The idea that the downtrodden of the earth should finally begin to receive a fair share of the profits of their labor is right. And the democracies have accepted it. The idea that men and women should be treated equally and given equal economic opportunity, which Lenin always emphasized, is also right."*

Under the brutal stewardship of misguided disciples, Marx's magnificent folly failed. History will have to classify this failure, which cost some 100 million lives, as one of the greatest human tragedies.

◆

What Snyder augured in 2017 (year the book was published) was already in evidence in an Amerika that had not changed but had revealed itself when Barack Obama was elected and reelected: an imperialistic, racist, xenophobic, misogynistic, and hopelessly obstructionist nation pretending puritanism while wallowing in scarlet promiscuity, a nation that, as it continues to veer to the right, is turning into a Mafia state. Snyder has eloquently and succinctly captured the essence of the inequities that plague Amerika and the world. *On Tyranny* is a book to be applauded, shared, and quoted.

◆

Science's assessment that *"we are on the road to destruction"* is accurate and supported not only by the madness of current events but by the Second Law of Thermodynamics which postulates that everything that has a beginning also has an end brought on by entropy — the gradual decline from plenty to scarcity, from order to disorder. Birth. Life. Death.

THOU SHALT NOT KILL — The sixth Commandment is being systematically desecrated by the loathsome *"Law of Retaliation"* — An Eye for an Eye, originally enshrined in the Mesopotamian Code of Hammurabi (circa 1754 BCE) and reprised with a vengeance in the Hebrew Bible.

Orlando Hall was put to death in Indiana yesterday by injection of pentobarbital. In ordering his execution, the Trump administration broke with tradition: An unelected incumbent must rescind all scheduled executions. Sentenced in 1995, the 49-year-old African American was no angel. He took part in the abduction, rape, and murder of 16-year-old Lisa Rene, whom he beat and buried alive with the help of accomplices. He was executed after a final appeal was dismissed by the Supreme Court. It was the first decision of the new justice, Amy Coney Barrett, a devout Catholic, who ruled in defiance of the sixth Commandment like the other five conservative justices in the nine-judge body.

Although Hall did not deny his role in Lise Rene's death, his lawyers claimed that racism had clouded the all-white jury's judgment. They argued that Hall's record,

"reflects the troubling racial disparities in capital punishment in the US where 45 percent of death-row inmates are African Americans, compared to only 13 percent of the overall population."

While nearly all states halted executions since the beginning of the pandemic, President Trump's administration has put to death an unprecedented number of inmates — eight since July — compared with three in the last forty-five years. Two more executions are planned in the coming weeks, despite a more than century-old custom that un-reelected presidents suspend executions until their successor is sworn in. Trump, who still refuses to acknowledge his defeat, seems determined to end his reign in a final, retributive orgy of blood.

The execution of Lisa Montgomery, a 52-year-old mentally ill victim of sex trafficking would be the first by the federal government in seventy years. Montgomery was convicted of strangling a Missouri woman who was eight months pregnant in 2007 and kidnapping her unborn baby. Originally scheduled for December 8, her execution was postponed until December 31, after her lawyers contracted Covid-19. The US also plans to execute Brandon Bernard, 40, on December 10. Bernard was convicted of the 1999 killing of two youth pastors in Texas.

Aside from its monstrous depravity, the most common and most cogent argument against capital punishment is that, owing mistakes or flaws in the justice system, innocent people have been and will inevitably be put to death. Witnesses, (where they are part of the process), prosecutors, and jurors can all make mistakes — or succumb to their prejudices.

While European nations have abolished the death penalty, the US, which has the world's high incarceration rate, continues to put people to death. According to Amnesty International, 130 people were sentenced to death in the US (which executes more people than have been found innocent since 1973 and released from death row).

Camus and Dostoevsky argued that the death penalty is unfair because the anticipatory suffering of the condemned before execution outweighs the anticipatory suffering of the victim of their crime. The continuous threat of execution makes the ordeal of those wrongly convicted particularly horrifying. Others have argued that the retribution argument is flawed because the death penalty delivers a *"double punishment"*: the execution itself and the anxiety-ridden waiting period. Many offenders are kept waiting on death row for long periods of time. According to the Washington, DC-based Death Penalty Information Center, the average time on death row in the US is eleven years. Things were made worse when the Supreme Court ignominiously refused to hold explicitly that the execution of a defendant in the face of significant evidence of innocence would be unconstitutional.

How does the state-sponsored assassination of a human being expiate the death of another except by gratifying the vilest urge to seek vengeance? Would it not serve society better to study the root causes and dynamics of aberrant behavior in the hope of reducing its incidence?

ACTING: A HEDGE AGAINST STAGE FRIGHT—I mourn the death of serious theater in Amerika, replaced by witless entertainment staged to produce a state of escapist euphoria in undiscriminating audiences that have lost the capacity or the will to think. It wasn't always so. When I arrived in New York in 1956, works by Edward Albee *(Who's Afraid of Virginia Woolf?)*; Lillian Hellman *(The Little Foxes)*; William Inge *(The Dark at the Top of the Stairs)*; Arthur Miller *(Death of a Salesman)*; Clifford Odets *(Waiting for Lefty)*; Eugene O'Neil *(Long Day's Journey Into Night)*; Thornton Wilder *(The Matchmaker)*; and Tennessee Williams *(Cat on a Hot Tin Roof; Suddenly Last Summer; Sweet Bird of Youth)*; drew eager crowds to the Broadway playhouses. Smaller, off-Broadway *"pocket theaters"* featured avant-garde experimental and absurdist plays that blended innovative works and futuristic production techniques. At the same time, works by Shakespeare and Chekhov, Molière, and Oscar Wilde, Maxim Gorki, Luigi Pirandello, and Eugene Ionesco drew large numbers of spectators to the classical stage. No more.

◆

I performed in several school productions, including *Hamlet, Le Bourgeois Gentilhomme*, Molière's scathing commentary on social-climbing by ignorant boors, and *Gringoire*, a dark comedy about the 16th century French ballad-monger who infuriated both the crown and the Church. I earned the praise of my teachers and hearty applause from the audience. Alas, the *"high"* that I experienced on stage was short-lived and did not arouse in me the urge to pursue an acting career. I had by then understood that living life involves a great deal of roleplay, pretense, and useful deception, and that I was neither suited nor inclined to assume other personalities when I already had a hell of a time being myself and accepted as such.

I would try again, half-heartedly, when I moved from New York to Hollywood in 1959, but the studio politics, clash of egos, and venomous rivalry put an end to this chimerical quest. A producer to whom I'd been introduced—he was chomping on a fat cigar at his mahogany desk—took one derisive look at me and said, *"You need elevator shoes."* I protested: Alan Ladd, James Cagney, Peter Lorre, Edward G. Robinson, Mickey Rooney, and … were considerably shorter than I. He reminded me that I was neither Alan Ladd, nor James Cagney, Edward G. Robinson, Peter Lorre, or Mickey Rooney. I conceded but asked him to explain the relationship between height and acting talent. He chewed on his stogie for a moment… and showed me the door. I have since delivered masterful performances as a hedge against life-induced stage fright. It's amazing how my award-winning impersonations have helped protect the man I really am.

♦

Sleet fell on parts of the Swamp yesterday. Nighttime temperatures dropped to near freezing. Stunned by the cold into a state of suspended animation, iguanas tumbled from trees. The Swamp: The Schizophrenic Climate State.

OILED, LOADED, AND COCKED—The US has a long and tragic history (now an epidemic) of mass shootings that began in 1922 but increased in frequency and lethality in 1966 with the massacre at the University of Texas in Austin. Since then, 2,000 people were killed, including 200 children and teenagers by 170 gunmen who were known to have violent tendencies or a criminal past. All but three were males. Nearly all crimes were racially motivated.

Amerika has always been the Wild, Wild West. It remains so to this day, thanks in part to a gun culture unique in the world, entrenched racism and xenophobia, and since Trump took office and cheered the hate mongers of the extreme right, a climate of permissiveness that has emboldened very angry and misguided individuals, some racists, some religious fanatics, to take justice in their own hands.

Amerika is a sick nation. It will take a massive social, intellectual, and cultural revolution to heal it. I don't see that happening any time soon. What I see is a steady rise in urban violence that could degenerate into insurrections and, possibly, a very bloody civil war.

◆

Snow vultures are not expected to swoop and invade the Swamp in droves this fall. The coronavirus stopped most of them dead in their tracks. It's been raining without respite. California boasts more sunshine in one day than the Swamp manages to deliver in a month.

UNINTENDED CONSEQUENCES — Sometimes cynicism helps ease the pangs of despair. Take the alleged *"positive"* impacts of the coronavirus, including the fictional decrease in global pollution. After all, cruise ships are in drydock, moorage or at anchor. Fewer jets are flying. Moreover, production of useless junk in China has risen, giving US *"entrepreneurs"* unequaled opportunities to scam consumers at home. Billionaires are getting richer and the stock market keeps soaring. Crowds are dispersing and thinning. Animals are venturing out of their lairs and reclaiming habitats that man purloined and poisoned with his presence. The virus, we tell ourselves, has done more to heal nature, at least temporarily, than Greta Thunberg could have ever dreamed. Not so fast. The coronavirus lockdown had zero impact on climate change. In fact, the concentration of greenhouse gases in the atmosphere surged to a new record high in 2020, even as the pandemic brought the world to its knees, According to the World Meteorological Organization, while carbon emissions fell during the spring, the drop amounted to little more than *"just a tiny blip on the long-term graph"* and will not have any meaningful effect on the atmospheric concentrations of greenhouse gases,.

♦

I was delighted to see diminutive but valiant Greta Thunberg gracing the cover of *Time* magazine. Trump must have been shitting bricks. Imagine, he was passed over as *Person of the Year* by a young girl who symbolizes and incarnates the dreams and aspirations of a new generation that speaks truth to power and dares to defy the status quo. I must dare to believe that the youth of the world can save it from itself.

I CALL IT MURDER — I weep at the death-by-wanton-execution of every animal, from squirrel and possum and prairie dog to deer, rhino, elephant, and whale, wolf, reindeer, and moose. Someone I know, an avid hunter (and hopeless right-winger) goes up to Maine every fall to hunt. He describes his blood sport as *"an act of charitable culling."* I call it murder. I keep reminding him that supermarkets sell meat, but he thinks he's doing animals a favor by sparing them the agony of dying of old age. I ask him, *"If you were an animal, wouldn't you choose to die on your own terms?"* He smiles sheepishly while loading his .223 Remington. I condemn hunting with one grudging exception: People who live in remote areas — the arctic, rain forests, and deserts where hunting is the only means of survival.

I also have an aversion for bullfighting which, other than football, bronc-busting, and bull-riding, is the most gruesome form of entertainment. I once told an aficionado (he considers bullfighting *"an art"*) that I'd endorse bullfighting if the bull agreed, in writing, to be mercilessly tormented and exhausted with banderillas, then slain and his ears and tail chopped off in front of an adoring crowd of imbeciles. He looked at me, his gaze narrowing as if my words betrayed stupidity or blasphemy, and he replied haughtily, *"You don't understand. A corrida is where virtuosity and courage are on display."* Right. It's also where idiocy and cruelty converge — the idiocy of the cheering spectators and the cruelty of a mortal elevated to godlike rank who enjoys torturing then killing an innocent beast.

A FEW DEADLY SINS — The punchline is that we are much less influenced by our DNA than by the conditioning — encoding? indoctrination? brainwashing? — to which we are subjected, from birth, by parents, teachers, *"spiritual advisors,"* the media, political propaganda, and social trends. We would all be different (had I been orphaned and adopted, say, by a devout Sikh family in Punjab, while an orphaned Sikh infant had been adopted by secular parents who lost nine-tenth of their relatives in Hitler's death camps). By now, I'd been concealing flowing tresses under a turban and sporting a long beard ... and he'd be spending the rest of his life wondering why Jews, like Sikhs, have been persecuted for centuries. What is wonderful to contemplate about this imaginary (but imaginable) scenario is that we're human, that we seek pleasure and have the capacity for pain; that we struggle with an existence that is neither always fair nor enjoyable; that we are designed to feel lust — none of us would be born without it; that we are prone to anger and sadness; that the distance between ambition and greed is minuscule; that envy can lead to attachment; and that a modicum of ego is essential to one's self-esteem. Surely, even rancor can be condoned if it doesn't kindle the urge to hurt others. Everything else is trivial automatism, habit, ceremonial, and convention. The least we owe each other is the sincerest acknowledgement that beneath all the accouterments we use to distinguish ourselves from others, we are all the fruit of Nature's boundless and mischievous creative forces.

◆

Of course, all knowledge comes at a price but not all people seek ... or accept the enlightenment that learning imparts. Some are perfectly content to live in the dark and breathe the noxious fumes of ignorance and blind faith. To learn, one must intentionally commit to unlearning the fictions we hold to be true. One great and common obstacle to knowledge is the conscious choice *not* to know. Ignorance is easily remedied by learning. Stupidity is incurable. We already live under a bubble of illiteracy, prejudice, and narrow-mindedness. Stupidity is universal and the disease is spreading on the wings of greed, fanaticism, and arrogance.*

---

* Stupid people, the late Berkeley University economics professor, Carlo M. Cipolla explained in his now famous essay *[The Basic Laws of Human Stupidity]*, share several identifying traits: They are abundant, they are irrational, they cause problems for others without apparent benefit to themselves and, confirming our worst fears: stupid people can and do rule the world.

A COLOSSAL JOKE—Coming from the Guardian, which I read and respect, I was surprised at the shallowness, the frivolity of an article by environment reporter Oliver Millman who, while focusing on the rising threat of global flooding, does not address the severe socio-economic problems faced by the areas and cities where he merrily urges people to relocate. It's as if he is so focused on inundations that he doesn't bother to address other factors, such as harsh winters, air and water pollution, overpopulation, depressed economies, high unemployment, poverty, and exploding crime rates. Buffalo and Cincinnati, where Millman urges people to move to, are predominantly African American cities. I know many white folks who would rather drown in a flood than cohabit with Blacks. This is Amerika. The Pacific Northwest, also on Millman's list, where it rains and rains and rains, is unaffordable and suffers from homelessness, rising crime, and violence. According to a recent hydrological survey, the Great Lakes are also prone to flooding as no effective containment measures have ever been put in place. Winters around the Great Lakes are long and bitter. There are apocryphal reports of men losing their dicks to frostbite while pissing in the lake during ice-fishing season. Moreover, none of the locales that Millman endorses has a favorable tax structure, and some are regularly devastated by tornadoes, blizzards ... and befouled by right-wing politics....

My recommendation? Move to high ground, say the mountains of Alaska, California, Colorado, New Mexico, etc. There is no risk of flooding there, but yahoos, nosebleeds, and chronic boredom are a fact of life. Seriously, everybody thinks that the Earth is this placid little blue marble in the sky when in fact it's a living, breathing, dynamic, geologically unstable, and climatically capricious internal combustion engine. Take away the threat of flooding, you still have seasonal monsoons, earthquakes, tsunamis, snowstorms, twisters, forest fires ... and the stinky effluvium of right-wing politics

Bottom line: We're royally screwed no matter where we live. Luckily, life is not forever so we won't be around to witness the end of the end. I feel sorry for the coming generations who did not ask to be born but, hey, that's the way the cookie crumbles. My mantra: Live life as if every day were your last and smile because it's all a fucking joke.

"A VERY STABLE GENIUS" — There is mounting speculation among scandalmongers and physicians, notably psychiatrists, that Trump might be suffering from *"the Great Imitator"* — neurosyphilis, the third and final stage of this dreaded disease. The symptoms of neurosyphilis are protean, varying widely from one individual to another. Common symptoms include irritability, inability to concentrate, delusional thinking, and grandiosity. Memory, insight, and judgment can become impaired. Insomnia may occur. Visual problems may develop, including the inability of pupils to react to light. This, along other ocular pathology, can result in photophobia, dimming of vision, and squinting. All these signs have been observed in Trump. Dementia, headaches, gait disturbances, and patchy hair loss can also be seen in later stages of syphilis.

Does Trump suffer from this condition? It's difficult to tell from a distance. There's a great deal of data we don't have access to which could be critical in reaching an ironclad verdict, including bloodwork and a sample of his cerebrospinal fluids. In Trump's case, there are many diagnostic possibilities, and we have scant background information because the slim medical summary he released is vague, unverifiable, possibly outdated, and probably ... doctored.

It is known that Trump was potentially exposed to syphilis based on his own admission that he was sexually promiscuous in the 1980s, a period when syphilis cases were rapidly increasing in the US. *"I've been so lucky in terms of that whole world,"* he told radio personality, Howard Stern, in 1997, referring to his dating life:

"It is a dangerous world out there — it's scary, like Vietnam. Sort of like the Vietnam era. It is my personal Vietnam. I feel like a great and very brave soldier."

Not to mention *"à very stable genius."*

If Trump has neurosyphilis, he'd be in famous company. Al Capone had it. So did composers Frederick Delius and Franz Schubert. Many others were suspected of having it, including Ivan the Terrible, Lenin, Hitler, and Mussolini. What might help to eliminate Trump from this group? Two simple blood tests, in combination, can determine whether a patient has syphilis now or had it in the past. If both tests are negative, then he doesn't have neurosyphilis. If one or both tests are positive, further evaluation, including a spinal tap, would be in order. The importance—both to Trump and the nation—of establishing or ruling out this diagnosis cannot be overstated, because this infection is treatable. Without treatment, however, the disease is progressive: It can make for a rather ugly end to one's life. In the absence of a conclusive diagnosis, a simple case of lunacy aggravated by meanness is what's left to explain the aberrant behavior of Amerika's 45th president.

DIVINE DECREE—No. You do not save the world by persecuting an already downtrodden minority. The Nazis didn't save it when they engineered *"The Final Solution."* And Jews won't save it by forgetting their past. Chastening Palestinians, stealing their dunams, bulldozing their homes, razing their olive groves and fruit orchards, erecting settlements on confiscated property, belittling or persecuting human rights advocates, basely equating the legitimate censure of Israel with anti-Semitism, slandering left-leaning Jews, misrepresenting a cruel military occupation as a path to security, and pursuing a one-state policy that will see Palestinians divested of their rights and ethnic identity will not endear them to posterity. The proposition that certain people have a right to a certain piece of land by *"divine decree"* is a sinister aberration, especially when that piece of land is wrested from its occupants by conquest and force of arms. Unchecked, all power lurches toward tyranny.

Israel is an ineluctable reality. I wish it long life, peace, and prosperity. I also beg Israelis to ponder one of the Talmud's most quoted counsels: *"Kindness is the highest form of wisdom."* It is also the most prudent path to lasting peace.

GROUND ZERO—The world is in turmoil. Where wars, skirmishes, and bloody *"pacification"* engagements are not raging, people are marching, demonstrating, protesting one thing or another, demanding this and the other ... but still devouring meat, driving gas-guzzling and smog-producing monstrosities, flying on air-poisoning jets, cruising on ocean-polluting ships, making babies, and pretending that life is forever. The world is awash in corruption, money laundering, treason, extortion, hunger, disease, and death. In short, it's a sinking Titanic. We must find consolation in the notion that, this time around, first-class and steerage passengers are similarly doomed. What happened to the Roman Empire, Babylon, classical Greece, Egypt, Persia, the Aztecs, Maya, and Inca is child's play compared to what is now in store. Meanwhile, the Doomsday Clock has been moved yet again and is now set at two minutes to midnight (ground zero of the impending global catastrophe).

◆

In the age of extinction, we are told, only love remains. Are we capable of loving indiscriminately? Or do we reserve our affection and devotion to those closest to us? We hear love being preached in houses of worship, these temples of mendacity where the fears and obsessions and hopes and chimeras that haunt us are stage-managed to produce jubilant hysteria or induce mournful self-contemplation. And we know that when the waving, outstretched arms that reach skyward come down, when the last amen, the final hallelujah have been uttered, when feverish eyes that glimpsed the face of *"God"* and sought salvation in a trance-like moment of ecstasy have reopened, the faithful, these pious souls, these model citizens, their ears still ringing from some exalted homily or sacred hymn, will reconnect with the profane world from which they come and the guzzling, the fornicating, the indiscriminate breeding, the gossiping, the hatred, the lying, the killing will resume.

I am not without compassion, but the feeling is abstract, not visceral. I'd be a hypocrite if I claimed that I can love anyone beyond the people in my life. And I'm not even sure that it's love. Age, I discover, has also spawned a persistent but guiltless aversion, a phobia for all manners of distractions and irritants: homicidal drivers; people who talk too much; people who talk with their hands; busybodies and know-it-alls; chauvinists and flag-waivers; selfie-takers, soccer moms, mystics, and religious zealots; cheerleaders and motivational speakers; the lionizing of sports figures; military parades; the Electoral College; *"states' rights;"* grits, sarsaparilla, and mint julep; spelling bees; marshmallows; televangelists; hog-calling contests; Tupperware parties; rodeos; football (violence and mayhem for the sake of violence and mayhem); wrestling (the vulgar, violent simulation of violence); NASCAR; hunting and bullfighting; people who start a conversation with *"So;"* golf, one of the most inane pastimes ever conceived; and hoity-toity pedants who like to say *"At the end of the day"* when what they mean is *"eventually,"* not late afternoon, evening, dusk, twilight, sunset or the dead of night. However irrational these phobias might seem, I shall not part with them. They enliven my existence.

Love? My friend Gurvinder says that the Gurus' wisdom can help turn ordinary humans into virtuous, divine-like beings. I know him to be righteous. He put his faith in the ferryman and crossed the river. I am still struggling to keep afloat in its raging current.

◆

I cried when I heard that a poacher in Africa had been killed by an elephant and then devoured by a lion. I cried for the elephant, cheered for the lion. Justice triumphed. I take no pleasure in this confession, nor do I feel a trace of shame. Yet deep down inside, I also recognize in me the distant, formless longing to see peace prevail in a world that has learned, at long last, not to hate. It's a yearning that has no future. I shall keep it entombed.

"GOD" **AND HIS ARCHANGELS**—The so-called "War on Terror," illegitimately launched after September 11, 2001 on bogus claims that Saddam Hussein had weapons of mass destruction, has since destabilized Afghanistan, Iraq, Lebanon, Libya, Sudan, Syria, and Yemen. It has killed hundreds of thousands of uniformed combatants and *"terrorists,"* and certainly an equal number of innocent civilians—*"collateral"* casualties, as the Pentagon likes to call them with a stupefying degree of indifference for life. Howard Zinn and Noam Chomsky have written copiously on Amerika's bulimic appetite for war. Should there be another one, they surmise, it'll surely be the last.

◆

One of Bob Mankoff's recent cartoons says it all: *"And so,"* concludes a chief executive officer at a stockholders meeting,

"while the end of the world scenario will be rife with unimaginable horrors, we believe that the pre-end period will be filled with unprecedented opportunities for profit."

"God" is money and his archangels are corruption, deception, and profits. Corruption is a highly infectious disease whose rewards seem far greater than its risks. I can't name a single country that has not succumbed to its siren call. Man is a corruptible creature, and temptations are many. Those of us who protest are denied entry into the capitalist heaven which is reserved for those who know how to play the game, namely the moneyed, the corrupt, the deceivers.

THE EYES HAVE IT — Well before we fry or drown in an ecological disaster, or are pulverized in a nuclear war inferno, we will lose every basic freedom, including privacy. The age of Surveillance Capitalism has dawned. A multitude of businesses are trying to get under our skin, steal our money, and subvert our soul. Samsung's smart TV records private conversations in living rooms everywhere. The latest Roomba vacuum cleaners map the user's floor plans. The GPS in your car or smart phone monitors every move you make. The CEO of Allstate Insurance hopes, in his own words,

"to sell the information we get from people driving around to various people and capture some additional profit source."

These companies belong to industries outside Silicon Valley's traditional purview of high-tech devices and Internet platforms, but what they share with Google and Facebook is the urge to generate profits from their intimate knowledge of our behavior, interests, and experiences.

These increasingly frequent invasions of our privacy are neither accidental nor optional; instead they're a key source of immense profits for many of the 21st century's most successful enterprises engaged in *"dark"* data extraction — with Facebook now considered the most wicked, the most deviant. It's *1984, Brave New World, Anthem, Fahrenheit 451*, etc., all rolled into one. But it's not future-bashing dystopian literature; it's here and now. There will be no need for mechanical robots. We are all being turned into helpless automatons in the service of capitalism.

BLAME THE VOTERS — Why? It's a question I've been asking since Trump was elected — and I have answers that any red-blooded Frenchman would have (and has since) loudly proffered but that few Americans in their state of catatonic vainglory would understand or tolerate.

- Pledging to *"preserve, protect, and defend"* the US Constitution does not prevent a president from bending the truth or lying through his teeth. They've all done it, from Washington to Trump.

- Lying is not always a prosecutable offense in Amerika although, paradoxically, calling someone a liar could invite a civil defamation lawsuit.

- Look at the voters, not the candidates, not even the incumbent. In France, the only country I can talk about with some semblance of authority, a man like Trump would not have been elected dog catcher, let alone head of state. French politicians who achieve a level of prominence are all highly educated, cultured individuals with prestigious academic backgrounds and professional achievements. And had he been, by some fluke, voted in, he would have been promptly ousted and interned in a psychiatric facility. Remember the small, ragtag band of peasants, hoboes, beggars, and petty thieves who, on 14 July 1789, helped topple a decadent, do-nothing monarchy, a slimy, toadying aristocracy, a venal, bloated clergy, and a corrupt merchant class? This single incident (followed by a few rolling heads) led to the absolute and irrevocable separation of church and state, the creation of a secular democracy, and the drafting of the Declaration of the Rights of Man, several provisions of which the US steadfastly refuses to sign or ratify to this day, including the Convention on Human Rights, which President Jimmy Carter signed in May 1977, the Convention on the Elimination of All Forms of Racial Discrimination, and the Convention on the

Elimination of All Forms of Discrimination Against Women. Considered inimical to political and religious conservativism, even the Convention on the Rights of the Child has not yet been ratified by the US.

- Keep your eye on the people, the culture—I mean the prevailing popular ethos—(or lack of it...), the phony prudishness and the abject lechery, the guns, the age-old propensity for violence, the exceptionalism, the racism, the xenophobia. I could go on. In France, a technically socialist republic that protects its citizens from the cradle to the grave with universal health care [France is first in world rankings, the US is No. 37 ...!], where college education is free, where the arts and sciences are generously subsidized by the state, where people enjoy a yearly one-month vacation, and where unions are powerful and quick to react ... if the government pisses off the people, the people shut the country down—or set it on fire.

Described as *"comically arrogant and out of touch,"* French President Emmanuel Macron, the *"president of the rich,"* tried to impose economic reforms that led to the Yellow Vests protests. Manifestly anti-labor and promoting tax cuts for the ultrarich, his initiatives would have weakened or eliminated the rights, privileges, and lifestyle perks to which the French are accustomed and which they will not give up without a fight. They fought and Macron backed down. It is difficult to understand how a country as violent as the US is unable (or unwilling) to engage in legitimate retributive violence but allows religion (and the NRA) to muscle in on the body politic. Macron, I am told, will likely not be reelected. Trump wasn't. Who is to blame if he had been?

PLANETARY FEVER—There's a smell of jungle rot after the rain, a fusty pong of decaying organic matter, part plant, part animal. When the sun deigns to show up, so do bellowing old men sporting gravid bellies and baseball caps. Looking as if they'd just come from the beauty parlor in their bouffant, hair-sprayed coiffures, the old women, trot to the pool clutching their Gucci bags, all decked out in their diamond earrings, Cartier watches, bracelets, anklets, baubles, bangles, and beads. Now buoyed on their pastel-colored noodles, they all woof and snigger at each other agitatedly with their hands in complicated patterns that do not match what comes out of their mouths. Picture a dozen partially submerged maestros, each conducting his own orchestra. Of course, they're not playing the same tune so what I hear is a cacophony of voices, accompanied by hand gestures, and wildly flailing arms sticking out of the water.

◆

Haven't seen the sun in almost a month. It's been miserable, cold, windy, rainy. Totally abnormal for winter in the Swamp. Local meteorologists don't know their asses from their piña colada. All their prognostications miss the mark. Warm fronts. Cold fronts. Squall lines and errant air masses. Convective currents. High pressure zones and low. Winds and gusts and flurries and seesawing dew points. Enough! They shower me with irrelevant data, pelt me with conjectures, and drench me with minutiae. And at the end of their endless soliloquies, I still don't know what tomorrow's weather will bring, which doesn't matter anyway because their forecasts are rarely accurate.

Worse, meteorologists never blame atypical weather patterns on the obvious: global warming and climate change. I phoned the local TV station's weather desk to ask why meteorologists never mention these phenomena as the probable cause of the cataclysms now engulfing Earth. They declined to take my call. I assume that they know the truth, that admitting publicly that the planet has a fever would be poison for the network and that even hinting at man's interference with nature would cause polluters in commerce and industry to call for the weather people's immediate dismissal.

BROOKING STUPIDITY—I reject the assertion that most people are alarmed by the consequences of global warming. Some may be intellectually capable of envisioning a bleak, broiling, arid, frozen, fallow Earth, but they quickly land back on their feet and exclaim:

> *"What are we supposed to do? Part with fossil fuels? Give up driving? Stop flying? Put a sudden end to plastics production and other petrochemical derivatives? Abstain from eating meat? The economy would collapse, and chaos would ensue."*

Hypocrites. These people care only about their personal wellbeing. Others argue, not without cause, that even if a few of the technologically advanced signatories to the Paris Accord heeded science's warnings, their efforts would be negated by nations whose emissions of toxic pollutants are greater than those of the US. You can diligently sweep your sidewalk every day but if your next-door neighbor is lazy and untidy your sidewalk can never be clean.

Life is brief and people, maddeningly, want to suck as much out of it as they can, and that involves satisfying their needs of the moment without restraint. The science of apocalypse is a distraction for which they have no stomach. You cannot enjoy life if you're constantly bombarded with news of your impending demise. Little, if anything will be done to effectively and decisively delay or annul the inevitable. Unlike animals, man is the only life form that places itself in the unenviable position of having to fix a self-created problem which it could have averted.

In the short term, we will be witnessing a growing—and frenetic—global south-to-north migration fueled not only by mounting civil unrest but by nature's retributive response to decades of neglect and abuse. One can only wonder why scientists who have come closest to the dire truth are the ones whose warnings are either ignored or violently rejected. Having said that, I think a political calamity will precede anything nature can throw at us. It's the merciful way out of the horrors that will follow. I smell War with capital W. It's a familiar odor, first sampled as a child, a mixture of gun powder, blood, the stench of fascism and putrefaction that never left my mind's nostrils.

◆

And lo and behold, the real cause of climate change was revealed by Republican Congressman Mo Brooks of Alabama, a white supremacist, who argued that [sic],

> *"Every time you have that soil or rock or whatever it is that is deposited into the seas, that forces the sea levels to rise, because now you have less space in those oceans, because the bottom is moving up."*

Now we know that climate change is caused by rocks falling into the ocean. What a smart man. It is the same sleazy mindset that must have prompted Texas Lieutenant-Governor Dan Patrick's imbecilic statement calling for the "reopening" of Texas by insisting that,

> *"there are more important things than living; lots of grandparents would be happy to give up their lives to keep the country afloat economically."*

Holy shades of *Soylent Green* (1973)*; and *Logan's Run* (1976).**

---

* It's the year 2022. Overpopulation, pollution, and resource depletion have forced leaders to tap new sources of nourishment for the teeming masses. The answer is Soylent Green--an artificial staple whose secret prime component is human flesh.

** Set in 2274, Logan's Run takes place in a city within an enclosed dome in what seems to be an idyllic society. There is little or no work for humans to perform, and inhabitants are free to pursue all of life's pleasures. There is one catch: life is limited and when you reach thirty, it is terminated.

As for the impending global disaster—war or ecological collapse—I have consciously decided not to think about it, to stop reading about it, to refrain from talking about it. Knowing that death is near will not prevent me from dying, so what's the point? All the warnings, scientific papers, seminars, conferences, scholarly symposia, all the huffing and puffing, all the handwringing, sighing, moaning, wailing, lamenting, all the anger and exasperation will amount to nothing. I spent twelve years in Central America warning against the evils of economic colonization, exposing human rights abuses, and advocating on behalf of homeless children, the poor, and persecuted indigenous minorities. Things are worse today than they ever were. All I earned for my hard work, my idealism, my dedication to the truth were a couple of death threats followed by the deafening silence of indifference.

THE MISINFORMATION AGE—Bloggers can be a wicked bunch. Some are morons. Others are agents provocateurs, planted troublemakers paid to refute inconvenient (verifiable) facts by subverting the truth or ridiculing the source. I was routinely subjected to ad-hominem attacks in response to a weekly column I wrote in a southern California daily newspaper. Letters to the editor were for the most part infantile, submitted by feeble-minded or grossly uninformed readers who just wanted to see their names in print, or penned by professional mind-manipulators (political "deprogrammers") whose reactions to my articles contained, in addition to strong rebuttals and vicious scorn, veiled threats. This is the new *"information age."* It's filled with ignorant imbeciles and a fifth column of ideologues, conspiracy theorists, and professional truth-deniers. I compare them to arsonists.

There is another problem: People don't read. Their patience for anything that requires concentration and critical thinking is waning. They have trouble focusing on anything that exceeds two lines of kindergarten-level content. Reputable publications are struggling to survive. Readership is down. Large photos and videos are replacing what were once pages filled with text. Another phenomenon is the climate of anti-intellectualism, anti-culture, anti-erudition that is spreading outward from the country's heartland and infecting new generations. Little will be done to reverse this trend.

The problem is multi-dimensional. First, the synergy between information overload, lazy, often inept journalism, and public apathy impedes vigorous and convincing coverage of the crisis. There's simply too much news out there and people choose to be tutored by news outlets that echo their political leanings and purport to serve their existential needs—mostly ideological and economic—rather than the truth.

Last, because people don't read and have lost the ability to focus, journalism has had to adapt and say as much as it can in a dangerously foreshortened format and amount of time. I remember when newspapers offered more in-depth coverage and analysis of events and ideas. Those days are gone. I will not say that this is a conspiracy; it's more likely a grudging adaptation to the exigencies of political correctness and advanced cerebral decay.

HALLELUJAH (AND PASS THE PLATE)—Sixty-five percent of humans believe in one deity or another. The same fraction also believes that after they're done trashing the planet and *"pass"* they will transit to a *"better place."* Religion has been fostering apocalypse as a logical end of its dismal existential model. Generations have been raised to welcome it, not prevent it. To them, the apocalypse is the logical finale to our earthly existence, a divinely mandated climax. After all, we will inherit a brave new world, at least this is what the Bible says.

Religion insists that there is a better world out there (somewhere near the Orion constellation or some other bright star system) teeming with pickup trucks, football, rodeos, beer, hog-calling contests, and triple cheeseburgers. Religion openly teaches us not to give a shit about this planet *("Thou art strangers in this world").* If we are on our way to our permanent celestial abode why bother protecting our earthly one? Religion and morality have always been at odds. As my old friend "Yevgeny" points out,

> *"Humans live in endless conflict between their primordial instincts and their irrational mind. Most use their mind to justify their primordial instincts, not to control them. Religion is a bridge between the two, helping to solve the cognitive dissonance between their impulses and reality. It does not work well! As any human construct, it is flawed."*

♦

Religion asserts that a talking ape has transcendental value in the Universe. While a talking ape is a fascinating phenomenon, stars will pursue their ceaseless cosmic journey until the end of time. Our value has been seriously overestimated. The Universe will do just fine without us. Everything is in a state of decay. We might just as well multiply, disfigure, and defile the Eden we were gifted, and precipitate the near extinction of all the bounties nature bestowed upon its greedy, venal creation.

A JEW NAMED JESUS — I read and reread an article written by a Paris-based American journalist who, while leaning on certain indisputable facts, echoes Israel's propagandist mantra, which is calculated to persuade Jews that they can be safe only in Israel. Citing the anti-Semitic blood libel pogroms of the Middle Ages — largely influenced by the Church and the Christian belief that Jews were collectively responsible for the death of Jesus — the article also mentions the Black Death which devastated Europe in the 14th century and gave rise to the common belief that Jews spread the pandemic by poisoning wells. In retaliation, some two thousand Jews were massacred in Strasbourg in 1349. The article summarizes the events that led to a ferocious wave of anti-Semitism during the Dreyfus Affair* and reminds readers of the thousands of French collaborators who sold France and carted its Jews to the gas chambers of the Third Reich. Last, it recounts the abduction, torture, and murder of a 23-year-old French Jew of Moroccan descent. There have since been scores of serious anti-Semitic acts of violence in France, incidents that Israel continues to exploit to prompt French Jews to immigrate. Few take the bait; many of those who do eventually return to France.

Anti-Semitism is not a French invention nor is it festering only France. According to the Anti-Defamation League (ADL), anti-Semitic attitudes have also surged in Poland, South Africa, Ukraine, and Hungary. And in the age of Trump, it has reared its ugly head in Amerika as well. Bomb threats, menacing messages on social media, and assaults on Jews have increased in recent years, according to researchers and federal data. The US saw a

---

* The scandal began in December 1894 when Captain Alfred Dreyfus was falsely convicted of treason. Dreyfus, a 35-year-old French artillery officer of Jewish descent, was sentenced to life imprisonment for allegedly communicating French military secrets to the German Embassy in Paris, and was imprisoned in Devil's Island in French Guiana, where he spent nearly five years.

record number of anti-Semitic incidents in 2019, the ADL reported, as it warned that extremists are using political fragmentation and the coronavirus pandemic to fuel further racial hatred. The ADL recorded 2,107 acts of anti-Semitism in the US that year, the highest number since record-keeping began in 1979. The cases included a sharp escalation in physical attacks. Said ADL chief Jonathan Greenblatt:

> *"This was a year of unprecedented anti-Semitic activity, a time when many Jewish communities across the country had direct encounters with hate. This contributed to a rising climate of anxiety and fear in our communities."*

High-profile attacks included a shooting at a synagogue in California, another in Pittsburgh which claimed eleven lives, a murder at a kosher grocery store in New Jersey, and a stabbing at a rabbi's house in upstate New York. Anti-Semitic incidents rose 12 percent from 2018, when there were 1,879 assaults, the audit found; 2018 was worse than 2017, which previously had the highest number of cases with 1,986. And 2019 saw a 56 percent increase in physical assaults, while harassment and vandalism also increased, the ADL said. Five people died in anti-Semitic violence and another 91 individuals were attacked physically, it added. More than half of the assaults nationwide took place in New York City, home to the largest Jewish population outside of Israel, including a large Orthodox community in Brooklyn. Incidents were reported in every state, except Alaska and Hawaii. Certainly, there have been many attacks on Jews in the US, many committed by mentally deranged individuals. They are the same psychopaths who attacked mosques (63 attacks in two years) across the US, killing many people. Several Sikhs, mistaken for Muslims, were beaten; at least six were shot to death in a frenzied display of nativist patriotism. They continue to be persecuted and assaulted because they sport long beards and wear turbans. Police brutality against blacks and Latinos is commonplace.

Attacks on Jews parallel the steady rise in violence in Amerika. Every day ninety-six people are killed and a few hundred injured by firearms. The homicide rate is thirty times higher than that of six European countries combined. Last year 13,366 people were killed, including 620 children.

Does anti-Semitism exist in France? Yes. Wasn't I recently warned by Jewish friends in Paris to hide the Star of David I have been wearing around my neck openly and fearlessly for years? The warning left me stunned. Does it exist in the US? And how! Can it turn as ferocious as it did in parts of Europe and the Arab world? Certainly. Could a Krystal Nacht take place in Amerika? Anything is possible, especially in what is still being touted (as was pre-Hitlerian Germany) as the most unlikely place of all. So far, none of my Jewish friends, particularly those who point to Europe as a hotbed of anti-Jewish hatred but turn a blind eye to anti-Semitism in the US, has expressed the slightest desire to abscond to Israel. They might want to reconsider.

♦

Anti-Semitism, like the clap, has always existed. One can argue that it began at the Council of Nicaea in 325 C.E. when Christianity became an *"official"* religion. Most significantly, this ecumenical conclave resulted in the first uniform Christian doctrine, called the Nicene Creed, a series of canons that furiously repudiate all the teachings that the Jew named Jesus dutifully followed,

One must dare to surmise that if the Jew named Jesus had not been born, anti-Semitism might be unknown. But then someone would have had to invent the Jews, someone to blame, to hate. Given a spurious pretext, often in the absence of one, anybody can hate the Jews.

SKILLS, NOT TALENT — It doesn't take talent to swallow razor blades, ride a unicycle up a flight of stairs, perform a card trick blindfolded, or dive into a bidet from twenty feet up in the air. All it takes is skill, practice, and the temerity to equate dexterity with artistry. It also takes balls to believe that anyone would be interested in such feats of inanity. I also know how an utterly talentless would-be performer can be turned into an overnight "sensation." Audiences would be aghast at the tricks a recording studio can perform to fool an uncritical — not to say philistine — public. Witness the thunderous bursts of applause and roaring standing ovations that *"singers"* on America's Got Talent (should be called Amerika's Got Skills because there's generally very little real talent on display...) are showered with. And while my beef is with the uninspiring quality of today's music, I am infinitely more critical of a new generation of singers, mostly female, who yell, scream, howl, wail, shriek, and ululate — the higher the pitch and the octave, they think, the greater their virtuosity. I won't insist that all vocalists sound like Luciano Pavarotti and Maria Callas, or José Carreras and the magnificent Jessye Norman. That would be too much to ask but I don't appreciate having my eardrums shattered by singers who rely on loudness and vocal contortions as a measure of their glottic skills. Give it to me straight, the way the composer wrote it. Don't embellish. Don't improvise. (I remember the diminutive Edith Piaf and pint-sized Charles Aznavour, neither particularly attractive, both attired in black, standing on stage motionless and singing their hearts out, performing their own compositions — superb melodies and intelligent, inspiring lyrics--real poetry). A talented entertainer doesn't need backup singers, pyrotechnics, long-legged, ass-grinding dancing girls, and barrel-chested goliaths who but for their pecs, biceps, and six-pack abs would be standing at the far end of an unemployment line. Wave a perfume-scented hand at a dog and he will recoil in horror. Offer him a steaming pile of dung and he will quiver with delight. Same with some audiences.

Sadly, hyperacusis (the result of trauma to my ears and a condition characterized by an acute intolerance to certain noises — vacuum cleaners, motorcycles, defective mufflers, sirens, and the sound of dishes clanging in the sink) has greatly diminished my forbearance for the kind of singing that elicits the orgasmic approval of contemporary audiences.

Though my musical tastes gravitate toward the classical, I also enjoy the Big Bands, jazz, blues, and the singers, male and female, who graced the airwaves and the stage in the 40s, 50s, 60s, and 70s. I think good pop music died sometime in the 80s and was replaced by mediocre tunes, idiotic lyrics ... and lots of screaming and howling. Where are Johnny Mathis and Perry Como and Frank Sinatra and Billie Holiday and Ella Fitzgerald and Nat King Cole and Rosemary Clooney, Andy Williams and Ricky Nelson now that we really need them?

SELF-CREATED DYSTOPIA—Several nations sank into Third World abysses after being seduced and bled dry by the siren call of *"communism."* The allure was compelling, the price was exorbitant. All the ills that will lead to the decline of other nations have their origin in a sharp turn to the political right, frenetic capitalism, xenophobia, and the comatose state of a once comfortable middle class on which they feed. A case can be made that it is the fate of all developed nations to turn into Third World wastelands while the poorest nations are submerged under an unsurvivable tide of indigence, famine, disease, and violence.

◆

Clear skies, radiant sunshine, and much cooler temperatures have returned to the Swamp. The next few nights should descend into the 40s (Fahrenheit), with the mercury dropping into the 30s at the Swamp's northern limits. Good sleeping weather. Yesterday I was perspiring. Time does not "flow;" we traverse it—in one direction and on a single-lane road lacking exit ramps or U-turns lanes. Nine months from now, if the road is clear, I will turn 84, a venerable age I feel in my bones but not in my mind. I keep working, observing. My craving for knowledge seems to be increasing as I get older. So much to learn, so little time left. In the interim, strangely, the facts I absorb no longer produce the anger or exasperation they once did. I am slowly learning not to give a shit. My abhorrence of the Swamp has not abated but abhorrence is a toxic emotion I must suppress for my own peace of mind. I don't know if it's the birth of wisdom or a gradual surrender to a reality I cannot change. Whatever it is, it seems to have calmed me somewhat. I miss my former self, but I have put him on hold. The intense phobias and passions of youth (we never lose them entirely) are slowly overtaken by a gentle weariness, followed by waning wanderlust and the courage to admit that we must endure the things we cannot change, including the specter of a dystopian world of our own creation.

IN THE NAME OF THE FATHER — I'm at the tail end of a 500-page book on the Holocaust, an event engineered by Germany and cheerfully aided and abetted by enthusiastic Russians, Ukrainians, Poles, Latvians, Estonians, Croatians, Romanians, Hungarians, and Slovaks. The book is a frightening reminder that the political dynamics currently playing out in the US provide the perfect synthesis and breeding ground for the revival and spread of fascism, neo-Nazism, and anti-Semitism. With Trump at the helm, with the psychopaths he kept on a leash (and the sycophantic cowards who dared not contradict him), anyone who says, *"It can't happen here,"* (with *"it"* meaning pogroms against Jews and systemic attacks against people of color — is hiding in a rabbit hole. It *can* happen here; it almost did as the Nazi Party rose to prominence in Amerika in the late Thirties and early Forties (it was known as the Bund). The organization cheered as news spread of European Jews being massacred. The Bund was opposed to US intervention in the Second World War, promoting instead a *"cordial agreement"* with Hitler's Germany. Father Charles Edward Coughlin, a Catholic priest, used his anti-Semitic radio rants to encourage support for Hitler's genocidal program. It is the same feeling (and agenda) that, with Trump's help, emboldened a growing number of right-wingers while fueling their hatred for anyone who is not white, Christian, straight, xenophobic, misogynous, and illiterate.

MAYBE, MAYBE—It is nothing short of astonishing that, after centuries of persecution, not to mention the bloody events in 1984, persistent harassment by the Hindu majority in India, and sporadic acts of violence against them in other countries, Sikhs still invest much hope in the goodness of men and the righteousness of human institutions.* I do not share their optimism but, after all, without hope, not much is left. Maybe, maybe if the gentle light of Sikhism could suffuse and illuminate the world, open the eyes of the willfully blind, and flush out the wax of ignorance out of the ears of the willfully deaf, maybe, maybe, we might all have a chance. *Maybe* is a word bereft of promise, an antidote to reality. I think therefore I doubt. A healthy dose of skepticism protects me from the baseless assumption that faith can result in the advent of the improbable. Faith often leads to unpredictable results, often regrettable ones.

---

* The 1984 anti-Sikh riots, also known as the 1984 Sikh Massacre, were a series of organized pogroms against Sikhs in India in response to the assassination of Indira Gandhi by her Sikh bodyguards. The ruling Indian National Congress had been in active complicity with the mob, as to the organization of the riots. Government reports estimate that about 2,800 Sikhs were killed in Delhi and 3,350 nationwide. Independent sources claim the number of deaths exceeded 8,000 and could have been as high as 17,000.

SMOKE AND MIRRORS—I find nationalism repugnant and frightening. Yes, Israel has the sovereign right and obligation to protect itself against any entity that would jeopardize its existence and security. This right does not extend to the persecution and debasement of an occupied minority. Supporting Israel and condoning its misdeeds because it's always been a friend of the US (on which it depends for its survival) is as offensive an excuse as it is aberrant. There is such a thing as a conspiratorial friendship—one that benefits the two sides but which, from an ethical standpoint, is immoral and pernicious. The US has been the grandmaster of mercenary alliances. It has aligned itself with villains solely as a means of promoting and protecting its own economic and geopolitical interests. For thousands around the world, that alliance has proved noxious, if not fatal. Consider the villains with whom Amerika has flirted: Fulgencio Batista (Cuba); Augusto Pinochet (Chile); Park Chung-Hee (South Korea); Islam Karimov (Uzbekistan); Saddam Hussein *"Our Man in Baghdad"* (Iraq); Rafael Trujillo (Dominican Republic); the Shah of Iran (and his CIA-funded murderous Savak secret police) who the US unceremoniously dumped when he got sick and became irrelevant. The list is much longer. That's the US side of the story. The Israeli side of this charade seesaws between a policy of targeted assassinations (more than 230 since the 1950s and resulting in at least 500 deaths—most recently that of Iranian nuclear scientist, Mohsen Fakhrizadeh); and grandiose schemes to achieve regional preeminence. The US and Israel have persistently lobbied to persuade Arab countries that their main enemy is Iran. The recent spate of ebullient Emirati-Israeli normalization initiatives has infuriated Palestinians and left them in a lurch.

The United Arab Emirates (UAE) insist its accord with Israel will benefit the Palestinians. A UAE spokesman has alleged that it will enable them to *"stand by the Palestinian people and realize their hopes for an independent state."* Nowhere in the document are the Palestinians mentioned by name. Earlier initiatives by Jordan offered full normalization of ties with Israel in exchange for an Israeli withdrawal from the territories occupied in the 1967 war. That initiative is all but dead.

◆

The *"Abraham Accords,"* as the treaty of peace, diplomatic relations and full normalization between the UAE and Israel is called, come after months of debate over Israel's stated threat to annex portions of the West Bank, a move that would prevent a mutually agreed two-state solution to the Israeli-Palestinian conflict from ever being reached. The Trump administration's January 2020 *"Peace to Prosperity Vision to Improve the Lives of the Palestinian and Israeli People"* outlines areas of the West Bank to be ceded to Israel, thus encouraging Israel to unilaterally annex those territories without engaging in negotiations with the Palestinian Authority or offering any concession in return. Smoke and mirrors. Somehow good history does nothing to erase bad history.

EPICURUS' ADVICE—I turned 83 in September 2020. Statistically, I'm closer to death, be it from old age, disease, an ecological disaster, or a nuclear holocaust, than people half my age or even 20 years younger. I don't fear death and I'm not afraid of living. Everything else is an annoying distraction. I live inside myself. Humanity's woes no longer interest me. I've done my part, and nothing has changed. Things are worse today than they ever were. The revelations and warnings of the scientific community are indeed alarming but little or nothing will be done to appease Nature's justifiable wrath. The Second Law of Thermodynamics suggests that humanity's existence is finite; it is preordained that being born is the first step on the journey to death. I read all the doomsday scenarios very carefully and I find myself yawning both at the indifference with which they are greeted and at the desperate obsession they arouse. At my age, and given all the turmoil I have experienced, it is quite permissible (and amusing) to just not give a fuck. I have been strongly urging some of my friends—as a hedge against premature insanity--to get off this tidal wave of apocalyptic portents and stop fixating on events over which they are impotent, which may never materialize, or which may take place when we are all long dead and buried (in my case cremated). If you have a roof over your head (many people are homeless); if you eat three square meals a day (millions are starving); if you live in a reasonably stable country (their numbers are declining); if you can still afford a few ostentations like wine, caviar, weekend retreats in the mountain, new threads every few months, and ferry rides to Italy's Adriatic Coast (while I eat sparingly and still wear the same clothes and shoes I wore 30 years ago …) then you are a happy, blessed man. Don't poison your existence. Take Epicurus' advice: *"Why should I fear death? If I am, death is not. If death is, I am not. Why should I fear that which can only exist when I do not?"* For my part, I have made peace with the inevitable. The end will come in one form or another, at a time of its own choosing, and my pronouncements will join the quadrillion words other critics and prognosticators have uttered in the bottomless cauldron of wasted breath. I'd be a hypocrite if I said I care. It's not easy to feel sorry for a species that insists on reproducing then sends its sons to war.

◆

Could it be that humans are genetically and irreversibly tainted, initially by their biogenic antecedents — great apes, whose chromosomes we share — and ultimately by the artificial social structures we set in place that bring about friction, strife, rivalry, and violence.? A tenuous status quo might have prevailed had industrialization not forever obliterated 200,000 years of hunting-gathering and bartering.

◆

Lousy, abnormal, violent weather here (and around the world) but not a single meteorologist dares blame it on global warming/climate change. A life of grinding monotony in the Swamp. Then there's Trump. The impeachment. The breakdown of civility. The polarization of Amerika. The ugly face of partisan politics. The debates, the lies, the ugly threats, the craven silence of toadying profiteers. Global anti-Semitism. The obscene rise in the cost of living. The shrinking Social Security benefits in defiance of an alleged *"booming economy."* My benefits will rise by less than $15 a month in 2021. That's the average price of a large pizza or two loaves of bread or a package of chicken breasts. It's one or the other.

◆

Now and then, for a laugh and an eagle-eyed look at human nature, I reread a hilariously prescient little book, *The Rise and Fall of Practically Everybody* by the late journalist/humorist Will Cuppy (1884-1949). In his witty dissections of the past (he pillories Nero and Cleopatra, Alexander the Great and Attila the

Hun, Lady Godiva, Miles Standish, and Lucrezia Borgia, Henry VIII, Catherine the Great, and Montezuma, to name a few), can be found the clues to the mess and afflictions these notorious personages handed down future generations. It will surprise no one to learn that victim of the meanness of men—he faced poverty and eviction—the gentle and witty Cuppy, aged 65, took his own life.

BY WAY OF THE TRILOBITES—Depending on current estimates, the Permian extinction took between 200,000 years and 15 million years to fully unfold. It was followed by two more extinctions—the End Triassic Extinction and the Cretaceous-Tertiary Extinction--both of which wiped out several species and created the necessary conditions for the adaptation of certain life forms and the creation of new ones. Given that an *"extinction"* (short of a catastrophic cosmic event or nuclear holocaust) takes a while to evolve, I wouldn't worry too much at this stage of the game.

Warning people of an impending calamity will not prevent it. News of an imminent disaster, however, has led to mass suicides: Masada, 73 C.E. (960 dead); Pilenai, Lithuania, 1336 (2,000 dead); Bali, 1906 (1,000 dead); Saipan, Japan, 1944 (10,000 dead); Demmin, Germany, 1945 (1,000 dead); Jonestown, Guyana, 1978 (912 dead); Waco, Texas, 1993 (76 dead); Rancho Santa Fe, California, 1997 (39 dead); The Solar Temple cult, 1994, (74 dead). Most people would rather live with false hopes than in fear of events they cannot curb.

The mechanics of extinction are staggering, almost incomprehensible. According to the editors of the Encyclopedia Britannica, the Permian extinction (also called Permian-Triassic extinction) was a series of pulses that contributed to the greatest mass annihilation in Earth's history. It was marked by the disappearance of over 95 percent of marine and 70 percent of terrestrial species. In addition, over half of all organisms present at the time vanished. This event ranks first in severity of the five major extinction episodes that span geologic time.

But the point is this: And so what! Does it really matter anymore? The mathematics of extinction are irrelevant so long as human population growth and overconsumption continue to drive the crisis. It is a foregone conclusion that we will all go by way of the trilobites, dinosaurs, and dodoes at some vaguely predictable future date. People did and do end their lives when faced with a calamity or dead-end existence. They are committing a form of mass suicide as we speak — subliminally — by procreating, eating like there's no tomorrow (while millions are starving) driving gas-guzzling vehicles, flying on poison-emitting jets, taking cruises on sea- and air-polluting ten-story ships, using pesticides, cutting down forests, dumping industrial waste into oceans, lakes, and rivers, just to mention a few of the crimes against nature that we commit in our bulimic quest for *"happiness."* Ironic, isn't it? In context, and given that nobody gives a crap anyway, does it really matter if final extinction takes ten years or one?

No one cares. Given that the *"end"* is near and unstoppable, submission is the wise man's choice. While I continue to take an academic interest in the subject, I'm not wringing my hands and lamenting mankind's fate. Nor can I in good conscience denounce the indifference I see around me as I find myself not caring either. I spent more than 60 years exposing corruption, greed, cruelty, hatred, injustice, and inequality. Eighteen volumes comprising some 700 feature-length articles, investigative reports, news analyses, and editorials line two shelves of my personal library. The upshot? Zero. I might as well have sat on my hands because nothing changed. Things in fact got worse, much of it due to the same crass collective indifference to corruption, greed, cruelty, and injustice. We are programmed to worry about the next five minutes of our lives, not about the next millennium.

At age 83, with my future well behind me and an unknown quantum of time still left, it would be unwise, counterproductive, and detrimental to my sanity to mope about the inevitable — my own death and the impending extinction (or putrefaction) of civilization.

For my part, I have made peace with the inevitable. The end will come in one form or another, at a time of its own choosing. Every moment is precious. It must be lived without obsessing over when, where, and how it will end. It is painful enough to know why. Life is a day-to-day affair. One of the secrets of longevity is to enjoy the moment—listening to Mozart; reading Nietzsche and Baudelaire, watching old classic movies, taking long walks, breathing mountain air, making love, confiding in friends, and keeping a positive attitude until the end because the end usually comes without warning.

FOR WHOM THE BELL TOLLS — *"Remember, democracy never lasts long. It soon wastes, exhausts, and murders itself. There never was a democracy yet that did not commit suicide."* So said John Adams (1735-1826), the second president of the United States. I can't tell if Adams, a haughty and politically ambitious man, championed democracy or despised it. Two centuries later, entropy, the inevitable process by which order leads to disorder, lends Adams' epigram a whiff of prophecy.

Yes, we divinize democracy, but we do almost nothing to defend it. Beguiled by the reverence with which we treat it, it relaxes, closes its eyes, opens its arms, spreads it legs, and soon gives birth to anti-democratic monsters and political con artists who usurp power and suppress all the freedoms that allowed them to hatch, mature, and embed themselves in society's skin. Busy living and procreating, the people wake up only when they have lost everything.

I no longer ask myself whether Donald J. Trump, a malevolent jester, ever respected democracy or if he even appreciates what it stands for. Not unlike his totalitarian counterparts in Argentina, Austria, Belarus, Brazil, Chile, Hungary, India, Israel, Poland, and Turkey, he fed on chaos, repeated falsities, and sowed fear. The coronavirus, a perfect pretext to quash dissent, further emboldened him.

♦

The pandemic that threatened to postpone the primaries resurfaced and deregulated the elections. This disruption disheartened voters, a prospect that Trump — who remarked that *"if anyone were allowed to vote, no Republican would ever be elected again in this country,"* and later warned that he would *"do anything to be reelected,"* — eyed lustily. He then threatened to cancel or postpone the November elections. He was already smelling defeat.

Even Trump's harshest critics can't blame him for the pandemic, nor a related economic collapse, nor four centuries of slavery, segregation, police brutality, and social injustice. The story of Trump's presidency, with its toxic mix of profligacy, cynicism, savagery, and vulgar rhetoric, has nevertheless led to this nexus. Taken together, these sparks, as we have just seen, have set fire to the powder keg.

Even as Joe Biden's inauguration nears, fears linger that the coronavirus, unemployment, bankruptcies, deportation orders, rampant racism, neo-fascism, and the confusion and anger that his nomination unleashed, could still lead to an insurgency.

Unhinged, dangerous, and polarizing, Trump is not the child who played with matches; he is the demented arsonist who wanted to scorch everything, especially democracy, the very institution that allowed him, despite his abysmal incompetence, and with the help of a clique of like-minded thugs, to desecrate it.

Those who still believe themselves protected by democracy cannot afford to ignore these disturbing signs. Speak out and you too can be the victim of police terrorism masquerading as *"protect and serve."* Resist and you too can be kidnapped in broad daylight, hustled into the back of an unmarked car, and disappeared. The road to fascism is paved with law and order. If democracy perishes, it is because we all pushed it toward the abyss. Never underestimate the ignorance or stupidity of people. They can make you rich and famous.

For whom the bell tolls? It tolls for us.

THE SHAPE OF THINGS TO COME — For more than half a century, my investigative journalism (the enemies of truth call it muckraking) focused on the absurdities and agonies of the human drama.

From 1994 to 2006, when my work took me to Central America, I wrote about the military juntas and corrupt puppet civilian regimes whose proxies routinely slaughtered street children and assassinated indigenous tribal leaders; governments that, with the help and encouragement of the CIA, resurrected death squads and murdered muckrakers; heads of state profiting from the drug trade and the trafficking of minors; grotesque political cartels whose leaders continue to live in luxury while the masses rot in misery. I said what I had to say and, yielding to scruples, not fear, refrained from saying more. My sole aim was to inspire, stimulate, stir, enlighten, tease, and infuriate. I succeeded in the moment, angering many, earning death threats in the process. But I failed spectacularly in the long term. Nothing changed. Instead, things got much worse. Outrage gave way to complacency, insensibility, and amnesia. The victims were asked to forgive the horrors they had endured in the name of *"national reconciliation"* and their tormentors have since retired to their estancias or been given political asylum in Amerika and dying of old age in Texas, Louisiana, and Florida.

Back in the US, I denounced injustice and inequality. I exposed the greed and moralizing hypocrisy of the religious right, a blood-sucking monster that burrows deep like a tick into the body politic and subverts it. I spoke of a system just as vulgar, fraudulent, and unfit as those I had denounced in the Central American Isthmus. And I never stopped railing against the two-party system (each party the flip side of the same tarnished coin, indistinguishable one from the other except in the partisanships and antipathies they inspire in their respective camps, both tied to corporate wealth, both intent on blocking reform in the name of capitalism, both beholden to Wall Street, the rich, and the powerful, both involved in immense larceny against people of color and the poor, both claiming to be the sole guarantor of democracy—while reinforcing the same legal vacuum and reactionary ideology that led to the rise of a Donald J. Trump and the villains who watched him rive the nation and profited from the chaos.

In 2012, after publishing several books, I decided to tell my own story, warts and all, away from the constricting injunctions of newspaper editors and impervious to the censor's red pencil. Spanning eight decades and four continents, this memoir is a candid, often irreverent polemic, a tribute to intrepid journalism, an homage to my tribe, and a window onto a world consumed with pedantry and false modesty.* I retooled it, translated it into French, and published it in 2019.**

♦

I don't have to dwell on the unravelling of Amerika and the sense of foreboding I feel about the future. Trump openly admitted that he would resort to dirty tricks to insure a victory in November. He even hinted that people in red states should vote twice—which of course is illegal—and urged *"citizen militias,"* feebleminded armed thugs to do his bidding. Being a *"patriot"* in present-day Amerika means you can shoot peaceful demonstrators and beat people who advocate wearing masks in public. Democrats are now being labeled *"socialist terrorists."* The pro-Trump propaganda has reached a fever pitch. This is not simple *"idiocy."* It's criminal insanity.

I never witnessed such a level of verbal and physical savagery as the last few months that marked Trump's

---

* A PALER SHADE OF RED: Memoirs of a Radical © 2012, CCB Publishing.
** JEU DE RÔLE: Souvenances d'un Baladin © 2019, CCB Publishing.

governance. The coronavirus is in large part responsible for the angst and anger that are sweeping the nation, but I also recognize the resurfacing of an unmistakably trait: bigotry, malevolence, and a natural predisposition toward violence. Thirty million people are unemployed. About four million are homeless. An equal number are behind prison walls, the majority people of color. The cost of living keeps rising. Food prices have increased between 11% and 30% since March. Thermometers and medical-grade alcohol disappeared from pharmacy shelves. Covid-19 continues to sicken and kill thousands of people every day; nobody really understands its etiology; no one knows how long it will linger; and an incompetent government, more interested in kick-starting a dying economy than saving lives, is adding to the chaos. The current pandemic may well turn out to be just the forerunner of many more self-inflicted scourges caused by man's ceaseless rape of his environment.

◆

We hope to bid the Swamp farewell. This is where many of my hostilities sprouted and, like killer vines, nearly suffocated me. I shall not miss it. Leaving it will help make the ugly truths I'm bound to exhume elsewhere more tolerable ... but no less worthy of scrutiny and censure. One last word: The less you pay attention to history, the more inclined you are to believe and parrot the lies it tells. The more sanguine among us believe that it is the fate of men like Caligula and Nero to pay for their crimes, if not at the point of a dagger, or at the ballot box, then from an assassin's bullet or strapped in a straitjacket and consigned to the padded walls of an insane asylum. Don't be so sure. History does not acknowledge that tyrants are a self-replicating breed. It surrenders that thankless task to philosophers and psychologists who know that in antiquity as on the very day this book is being published, tyrants proliferate like viruses and do not go away on their own. They must be liquidated.

THE FINAL CURTAIN — Even as a child, when hounded by the Gestapo, fleeing from one hamlet to another, and living in suitcases for ten years following the end of WWII, I sensed that the future is not a separate and quantifiable dimension but the predictable if uncontrollable extension of a fleeting *now* which, by the time you reach the end of this sentence, will have swiftly receded into an irretrievable *then*. I have also long held that mankind is an unrepeatable evolutionary oddity destined, thanks to an imbedded insanity gene, to slog toward self-extinction. The only things that have changed since the prehistoric times are the means to accelerate this process. Dimly perceived when I was a boy (the Germans had invaded France, my father had been arrested, beaten, and imprisoned by the Gestapo, and I'd narrowly escaped Hitler's extermination factories) the realization that liberty, equality, and fraternity — France's audacious but fragile motto are fanciful objectives-- came into clearer focus when I attended my first theater performance.

"I'd rather live without hope than nourish a dream that can never be," I mused as the curtain came down halfway through August Strindberg's tragedy, *A Dream Play*, and as theater patrons snaked through the aisles toward the lobby during intermission to stretch their legs, wet their whistles, empty their bladders, expel some gas, grab a smoke, and talk over each other until the buzz of several hundred voices crested to an incoherent drone.

Swedish playwright Strindberg's tragedy argues that *"human beings are pitiable;"* that *"every joy must be paid twice over with sorrow;"* and that humanity's only reality is the endless repetition of *"duty and sin and guilt."* I was fifteen when my parents took me to see this strange and troubling drama. I remember how stunned I was to discover that the same insights, doubts, fears, and antipathies awakened in me at an early age by a succession of life-altering ordeals had been so vividly rendered, more than three decades earlier, not in a work of philosophy or a morality play but in a stage production created to tell the world that life is an illusion and that dreams can never come true.

Written in 1901, the play takes audiences on an anguished journey into the unconscious mind. Foreshadowing the anxieties, misgivings, and horrors that would soon engulf the world, it nimbly echoes some of the convulsions, obscenities and crimes that disgraced and bloodied the pages of history in the decade preceding the dawn of a new century. Surely, Strindberg must have been mindful of these upheavals as he devised the plot and imparted his characters with their wraithlike existence.

In writing *A Dream Play*, which he called *"my most beloved play, the child of my greatest pain,"* Strindberg said he attempted to,

"... imitate the inconsequent yet transparently logical shape of dreams. Everything can happen; everything is possible and probable. Time and place do not exist; on an insignificant basis of reality, the imagination spins, weaving new patterns; a mixture of memories, experiences, free fancies, incongruities, and improvisations. The characters split, double up, multiply, evaporate, condense, disperse, and re-assemble. But one consciousness rules over them all, that of the dreamer; for him there are no secrets, no scruples, and no laws. He neither acquits nor condemns, but merely relates; and, just as a dream is more often painful than happy, so an undertone of melancholy and of pity for all mortal beings accompanies this flickering tale."

Agnes, Strindberg's protagonist, is a daughter of the Vedic god Indra. She descends to Earth to bear witness to the evils perpetrated and endured by mortals. She interacts with dozens of characters, some of them having clearly a symbolic status, including four gurus representing theology, philosophy, medicine, and law. After experiencing all manner of human indignities — poverty, materialism, class struggle, persecution, and the grinding routines of family life—Agnes concludes that human beings are to be pitied. She returns to the cosmic realm from whence she came and awakens from the dream-like sequence of events, realizing that she too had become caught up in their nightmares.

The *"nightmare,"* I construed as the final curtain came down, was the antithesis of a universal dream whose features were at that time unclear—more Quixotic than rational. The stirring counsel in the Kabbalah would come to mind as I later mused over the play:

> *"In life you don't get all the answers at once. First you must absorb and live with one simple truth. Then later you must find another truth, one that may seem to clash with and negate everything you previously knew. Then, from that confusion, emerges a higher truth—the inner light behind all you had learned before."*

◆

I would later be taken to see Anton Chekhov's play, *The Seagull*, which first opened to rave reviews at the Moscow Art Theatre in 1895 and which may have inspired Strindberg. Chekhov's drama conveys modern man's inability to find his *"place."* It exposes his subconscious yearning to be *"elsewhere,"* and unmasks his painful sense of squandered dreams and denied hopes. Characters are dissatisfied with their lives. Some long for love. Some yearn for material riches. Some crave recognition. None, however, ever seems to attain happiness.

Written in 1882, *An Enemy of the People*, by Norwegian playwright Henrik Ibsen, which I read years later, is the story of how brave men who dare to speak unpalatable truths can survive overwhelming odds. The play slams democracy for its compliant tolerance of undemocratic institutions. On one hand, leaders are at the mercy of a tyrannical majority; on the other the governed are afraid of risk and are too stupid, greedy, conformist, or spineless to rebel.

I have since sought, found, and rejected other truths. I redefined the nightmare as an attempt by ideological storm troopers to undermine democracy, to misinform, to poison the national debate with sordid lies and ethnocentrist prattle disguised as patriotism, and to impose their will and promote social, cultural, religious, and political standards that, instead of inspiring dreams, spawn unspeakable hallucinations.

♦

No one listens to the truth. The more shocking it is, the deeper we bury it. I read somewhere that the US plans to spend $1.7 trillion to rebuild every component of its nuclear arsenal to counter Russian and Chinese nuclear stockpiles. The madness of the Mutual Assured Destruction strategy of deterrence diabolically disregards the horrors wrought by a Pyrrhic victory. Unless it comes first, fast, and furious, the Great Ecological Collapse will seem like a walk in the park compared with the looming atomization of man by man.

PARTING SHOTS — Writing in 1990, historian Charles L. Van Doren (1926-2019) prophesied,

> *"By 2010 there will be few nations that do not claim to be democratic, and moreover try to be. But it is conceivable that this could turn out to be the high tide of democracy, the preface to its eventual defeat."*

Van Doren warned that the greatest danger to democracy comes not from the totalitarianism of left or right, but from democracy's oldest and most persistent foe — oligarchy, the rule of the few over the many for the sole benefit of the few.

In a tale, as in a revolution, the most difficult part to invent is the ending, especially when predictable scenarios exceed the limits of imagination. Storytellers must not only have a flair for history; they must own up to it. An ending is not supposed to be a surprise. To envision the kind of ominous climax suggested in my play, *One Last Dream* — that creation's payback is extinction — readers must also reflect on the paroxysms of lunacy and violence that lend it credence, that are apt to hasten it. One facet of madness is the willingness to kill, or die, for an idea.[*]

It is not improbable that well before we fry, freeze, or drown in a Biblical flood, we will be pulverized, by design or miscalculation, in an atomic inferno. It is also not inconceivable that halfway between an ecological disaster and a nuclear holocaust we will become the servile pawns of a new hereditary aristocracy, a tiny handful who own everything while the rest of us spend our lives toiling for them, paying them rent, and never getting ahead.

The Third Law of Thermodynamics (entropy) applies to human wisdom as well as to the material world. Both are in a state of anticipated decay, a condition that has fostered the

---

[*] One Last Dream, © 2012, CCB Publishing.

advent of oligarchic elites. The erosion of parity is the predictable result of deliberate policies designed to harden capitalism's stranglehold. Only socialism offers the motor force of an equalizing countertrend. And only greed, selfishness, willful blindness, and stupidity will prevent its advent.

◆

The correlation between political leanings and cultural attitudes is becoming ever more evident. By stoking the fire, Trump corralled a share of voters who harbor racist, sexist, and xenophobic views. He deliberately exacerbated Amerika's divisions but even after losing the election his vision of national identity will remain on a collision course. Years of rising, bubbling discontent, turbulence, and retributive violence cannot be ruled out.

◆

I turn the pages and peel memories like an onion. Post-war Amerika: industrious; affluent; smug; secure in its hypocrisy and crippling delusions; bursting with hope, brimming with opportunity. A family of four lives comfortably on one wage earner's salary. The dollar has weight and worth. *"Made in the USA"* spells excellence. A car costs $2,000; a gallon of gas — 23 cents. You can buy a decent house for $22,000. Sensing that foreign policy is strictly about power and narrow interests (whereas a growing right-wing fringe deems values and morals to be for the feeble-minded) President *"I like Ike"* Dwight D. Eisenhower warns against the evils of the military-industrial complex and the lure of armed entanglements, while economists and social scientists caution against the very excesses that, six decades later, would turn the US into a mafia state dedicated to enriching a privileged few by emasculating a once thriving middle class. If a system is built on power but lacks legitimacy, behaviorists warned, it will destroy itself. If it asserts moral truths but lacks the power to enforce them, it will unravel. Their counsel fell on deaf ears.

Amerika is no monolith. Viewed from a safe distance, however, it matches the caricature-like image much of the world has formed: a nation that forswore all princes and potentates in exchange for the majesty of self-rule [but which capitulated to the czars of capital]; a theocentric nation hooked on triumphalism, given to gluttonous mercantilism and bulimic consumerism, a goliath beguiled by its grandiose self-view and readily seduced by the idolatrous slogans it keeps coining in its own name; a hulk obsessed with bigness: super-sized meals; wall-sized television screens, monster trucks; jumbo jets; mega churches, mammoth sports arenas, epic political rallies at which the voices of thousands of transfixed flag-wavers rise is a single, thunderous roar of delirious, hate-tainted jingoism.

Of Amerika, I deduce a sanguine, gregarious, and resourceful people prone to frivolity and hero worship. Alas, they don't worship the gods of knowledge and culture. Instead, they deify thespians and crooners, many of dubious talent, fictional celluloid *übermenschen*, comely people and sports figures, most of them mediocre human beings who but for their height, brawn or dexterity with some implement, would be living in obscurity instead of earning obscene wages.

At their finest, individually, Amerikans are the most generous people on earth. At their worst, they are annoyingly trivia-driven, provincial, blinkered, outwardly cocksure, inwardly skittish, overindulged, overfed, and oversexed. The men are high-strung, homophobic, sexually conflicted, and truculent. Bursting with testosterone, they are desperately protective of their masculinity, enamored of their pickup trucks, and enraptured by their guns, which they keep lovingly oiled, loaded, and cocked. Women are prematurely pubertal; as they age, many develop neuroses resulting from forced long-term exposure to Amerikan men.

To those who suggest that Amerika has changed in the past 65 years, I submit that it is just more *revealed*: It was always a charismatic fraudster; it eventually bared its vulgar soul when Barack Hussein Obama ran for president, was elected, and reelected for a second term. Who can forget protest signs showing a white-faced and bloody-mouthed Obama as a satanic clown, or as Hitler, complete with mustache and swastika? How odd that burning the flag infuriates red-blooded patriots, but depicting a sophisticated, refined, urbane president as a buffoon and a maniacal fascist is hailed as *"free speech."*

The ugly aftershocks and secessionist rants that Obama's victories generated, the deep current of racism coursing through Amerika's veins, suggest that large numbers of its citizens are prejudiced, xenophobic, anti-progressive, misogynous, and dementedly religious. The November 2014 mid-term elections, in which six of the most backsliding states helped Republicans regain control of the Senate, tend to validate that premise. In Amerika's first black commander-in-chief, they now saw a symbol of that nation's increasing diversity and transformation that scared the hell out of them. The potential for racially motivated violence was never higher, as mushrooming far-right terrorism and a string of police-involved incidents would demonstrate. They didn't like Obama because he's Black; they elected a predator who dyes his hair and wears orange makeup.

MEANWHILE, BACK AT THE SWAMP—Were it not for a Herculean and costly effort to maintain, repair, upgrade an infrastructure vulnerable to the elements—heat, humidity, sea erosion, torrential rains, flooding, and an occasional hurricane or two--the Swamp, a flat, featureless, topographically uninspiring, overly urbanized expanse, would soon revert to the fetid, malaria-infested fen it was before conquistadors and land speculators took it over and turned it into an air-conditioned winter haven for the geriatric set. The Swamp is spending $500 million to address its most vulnerable districts by raising roads and installing pump stations to shore up flood-prone areas. Sea levels are projected to rise by as much as six feet in the coming years. Switching from septic tanks to a region-wide sewer system is estimated to cost an additional $4 billion.

◆

After several days of exceptionally frigid temperatures, the mercury is slated to climb to 90F by tomorrow. As infections and deaths from Covid-19 continue to soar, and as the nation prepares, prematurely perhaps, to test the efficacy of several vaccines, a cure against Trumpism is nowhere in sight. Like the hydra, Trump's legacy has the capacity for spontaneous and indefinite self-renewal. Cut one arm off, two grow back. Seventy-four million voters, creatures capable of movement but not of rational thought are poised to bestow Trumpism morbid immortality. Woe.

MONSTERS AND CONTORTIONISTS — *"All the world's a stage, and all the men and women merely players: they have their exits and their entrances; and one man in his time plays many parts, his acts being seven ages."*

From preacher's pulpit to school bench, the link between the order of nature and the structure of society is upheld. There is, we are told, a cosmic hierarchy, with *"God"* at the summit, followed by angels, saints, men, and beasts. We are led to guess that, at the same time, there is also a social ladder dominated by monarchs, corrupted by plutocrats, conned by the clergy, defrauded by the merchant class, cheapened by the populace, and redeemed by those who are indebted to no one. Everything is staged.

Every morning when we wake up, we disguise ourselves, rehearse our lines, recreate the character that responds to other people's expectations of us, and we scramble back on stage. Husbands and wives mime roles for which they are ill-prepared, if not inapt. Children play at being sons and daughters, cowboys and Indians, cops and robbers. Teachers pretend to be pedagogues. Coerced by *"God,"* Moses, the heartless inquisitor, the bloody autocrat who brought on plagues and the flames of hell upon those who granted themselves the right to communicate directly with YAHWEH, plays lawmaker and avenger. Roused by the messianic rapture that the Roman invasion awakens among the Jews of the ancient Davidic kingdom, Jesus grants himself the role of *"Savior."* Pontius Pilate plays governor of Judea; Tiberius plays emperor. Crusaders and Inquisitors pillage, burn, and kill; their victims are anonymous extras that the directors relegate backstage. Prophets, mystics, popes and "princes" of the church are the protagonists in an absurd spectacle that separates them from mere mortals. Kings and queens, all looters, usurp the rights of the people and play overlord; their subjects have fun being their vassals.

Hitler played at being Hitler, Mussolini interpreted Mussolini. Stalin, Mao, Pol Pot, Ceausescu, Saddam Hussein, and the Kim dynasty, their diabolical ambitions unsated, jumped on the bandwagon. Joseph McCarthy, a drunk and a liar bursting with hatred toward those who, by his grotesque standards, did not submit to Amerika's metaphysic—unbridled capitalism and stilted patriotism—pretended to be a senator. Raped when still a child, Norma Jean, the adorable young woman played all the roles a heartless Hollywood dictated when they renamed her Marilyn Monroe—except her own. Historians toy with the past and modify it when they can. Soldiers play war; the police and bandits indulge in roles that often merge. Politicians pretend to represent their constituents while selling their soul to the highest bidder. Even whores have more dignity. Bankers play Monopoly with other people's money, lending it at usurious rates and paying miserly interest. The clergy fools the faithful who play the game of "saved souls." Deaf, mute, and blind, *"God"* plays hide-and-seek in his imaginary domain. Daddy played doctor and mommy played housewife. When they died, mourners faked grieving, went back home, ate, napped, defecated, fucked, and played at life until it was their turn to die. It's all an immense, rib-splitting, heartbreaking buffoonery, a carnival where jugglers and magicians, contortionists, and monsters swarm. To unmask them all and to talk about them out loud, I played journalist, the role that would allow me to recognize and exonerate myself.

◆

Everything we know we learn by osmosis. We don't invent anything. Our reasoning is very rarely original. We regurgitate like parrots what our parents force-feed us, what our teachers drum into our skulls, what the clergy sermonizes as it pretends to be saving our souls, what we distill under the influence of prejudices or immovable ideas that are not our own, from a history that we haven't lived, and from what society forces us to swallow if we do not want to be ostracized.

◆

When Candide is quoted as saying *"We must cultivate our garden,"* Voltaire rails against optimistic philosophers who claim that *"everything is for the best in the best of all worlds."* Candide, who witnesses all forms of wickedness during his adventures, also denounces intolerance, prejudice, superstition, and the evils of authoritarian rule. He also urges us to set aside metaphysical issues and deal instead with things that can be changed— working to heal an ailing world and make it better.

Tersely concluding his novel with that now famous exhortation, Voltaire leaves the reader suspended between hope (the illogical belief in the occurrence of the implausible) and healthy cynicism.

ACKNOWLEDGEMENTS—I am indebted to my parents, learned, urbane, fair-minded, for instilling a love of books and an appreciation for music, art, and philosophy, for sparing me the enslavement of religious indoctrination, and for enduring, if not always endorsing, my wildest antics. To my mother, a selfless, unassuming, cultured woman of great refinement, I owe my fondness for the beauty and symmetry of nature. From my father, a loving, iron-willed and incorruptible man who abhorred ostentation and pretense, I learned that self-esteem and a reverence for truth bestow infinitely greater rewards than money or material comfort.

I salute my teachers, those I pleased when I applied myself and those I exasperated when I didn't. Their erudition, pedagogical skills, and saintly patience for the lazy, unfocused, mercurial, and rebellious student I was helped lay the foundations on which I would erect a lifetime career of endless beginnings.

I can never sufficiently acknowledge the immense influence several writers, poets, and philosophers had on the constantly evolving person I would become and, by extension, on the ideas I would champion. Their prose, verses, insights, and eye-opening reflections resonate as intensely today as they did in the days of my youth. Most were French. One was denied a Christian funeral for penning vitriolic anti-clerical tracts. Four were imprisoned, the first for denouncing the bestiality of colonialism; the second—the son of a prostitute—for *"vagabondage, lewd acts, and other offenses against public decency;"* the third for stretching the limits of literary freedom in pamphlets that mixed raw eroticism with civil disobedience. The fourth spoke for the common man and rose with uncommon bravery against the corruption of the clergy and the decadence of the military establishment.

Three were Russian. One of them, a novelist, essayist, and journalist, explored human psychology in the social, political, and spiritual milieu of his time. His works are populated by neurotics and lunatics, the kind who become pope, king, dictator, tyrant, president. The second, a ruthless satirist, imparts surrealism and the grotesque with an unusual aura of normality. The third, the one that struck me most, was a Freemason [like my father, and later like me], a *"professional revolutionary,"* and theorist of anarchism influenced by Hegelian thought.

My other mentors wrote in Arabic, English, Dutch, German, Sanskrit, and Spanish. Three hailed from Ireland; one did not survive the spurious puritanism of his Victorian milieu. One died insane — as do those who seek shelter from the battering storm of reality in the sanctuary of delirium. The third was excommunicated for trying to resolve the conflict between religious dogma and secular knowledge, and for departing from Aristotelian thought by emphasizing the depth of human ignorance. All were free thinkers, rebels, defenders of secularism, all long-deceased but whose heterodoxy and reformist ideas still inspire new generations of resisters, heroes, and martyrs. All were iconoclasts, now long dead, but whose works and the reformist ideas they conveyed still inspire new generations of mavericks-in-training.

It is with equal reverence that I thank my friends, few as they are, attentive and faithful, whose encouragement supported me during difficult moments of introspection and self-criticism during the gestation of this work.

I must also salute some readers, especially bloggers and social media fans who spinelessly assault me while draping themselves in anonymity. The vitriol that my writings inspire reinforces my conviction that in this era of lies and unreason all opinions have equal weight but that only the truth, rare and easily distorted, uncomfortable, and often cruel, must prevail.

One exquisitely and succinctly framed truth can be found in "Yevgeny's" most recent e-mail. He writes: *"You are like a tree that was planted in the wrong place."* Yes, a rootless tree whose withered limbs stretch longingly to a past without a future.

♦
♦ ♦

Born in Paris, W. E. Gutman is a retired journalist. A former writer at the late-great futurist magazine, *OMNI*, and an ex-press officer at Israel's Consulate General in New York, he reported from Central America from 1994 to 2006.